Cricut Maker

A Comprehensive Guide to Mastering Tools

(Complete With Diy Project Ideas and Practical Steps)

Steven Brown

Published By **Oliver Leish**

Steven Brown

All Rights Reserved

Cricut Maker: A Comprehensive Guide to Mastering Tools (Complete With Diy Project Ideas and Practical Steps)

ISBN 978-1-77485-458-7

All rights reserved. No part of this guide may be reproduced in any form without permission in writing from the publisher except in the case of brief quotations embodied in critical articles or reviews.

Legal & Disclaimer

The information contained in this book is not designed to replace or take the place of any form of medicine or professional medical advice. The information in this book has been provided for educational and entertainment purposes only.

The information contained in this book has been compiled from sources deemed reliable, and it is accurate to the best of the Author's knowledge; however, the Author cannot guarantee its accuracy and validity and cannot be held liable for any errors or omissions. Changes are periodically made to this book. You must consult your doctor or get professional medical advice before using any of the suggested remedies, techniques, or information in this book.

Upon using the information contained in this book, you agree to hold harmless the Author from and against any damages, costs, and expenses, including any legal fees potentially resulting from the application of any of the information provided by this guide. This disclaimer applies to any damages or injury caused by the use and application, whether directly or indirectly, of any advice or information presented, whether for breach of contract, tort, negligence, personal injury, criminal intent, or under any other cause of action.

You agree to accept all risks of using the information presented inside this book. You need to consult a professional medical practitioner in order to ensure you are both able and healthy enough to participate in this program.

TABLE OF CONTENTS

Introduction 1

Chapter 1: What's A Cricut Machine? And How Does It Function? 3

Chapter 2: How To Set-Up The Cricut Maker Machine 23

Chapter 3: Everything You Should Learn About Cricut Design Space 30

Chapter 4: What Can I Do With Cricut Machine? 51

Chapter 5: How To Create A Business In Cricut? 71

Chapter 6: How To Earn Money With Your Cricut 93

Chapter 7: Where To Sell Items You've Made By Your Cricut? 118

Chapter 8: Project Ideas 133

Chapter 9: Maintenance Of Your Cricut Machine 151

Chapter 10: How To Start Marketing Your Product 163

Chapter 11: A Look At Cricut Maker Machine . 170

Conclusion 181

Introduction

You've probably heard from your colleagues about Cricut or perhaps you have the Cricut machine at home. The machine was offered to you as a gift and you're not sure how to begin. But don't worry because you've picked the perfect beginner's guide.

Everyone around the globe who are interested in making and crafting are very familiar using Cricut and its creative cutting machines. For machines for cutting dies, sometimes referred to as art plotters, cutting plotters machines Cricut is the best well-known brand name. It is a great tool for simple crafts such as scrapbooking or other crafts, such as creating christmas decorations which are complex.

This book will explain how home-made die-cutting machines are designed to cut paper, vinyl silk, as well as over 100 other materials we'll cover.

Particularly due to the style, the Cricut machine could be similar to printing. However it's not a printer. Cricut machine won't have the design printed. Instead, the design will be cut using the materials you're making use of. Thus, on your screen, you'll make a pattern, and the machine will take the paper, cloth or cardboard, vinyl and even the most bizarre material from it. The template can be printed on any type of material of your choice employing any of Cricut versions.

Chapter 1: What's A Cricut Machine? And How Does It Function?

The Cricut is a machine for cutting. It is, at the very least, is the correct word. But it doesn't even begin to define the vast potential that this device has. I have Cricut Maker, which is the Cricut Maker, currently the most powerful machine of the Cricut Maker series. It is with the Cricut Maker you can do nearly everything: cut various materials, customize t-shirts sewing projects postcards, birthday invites banners, lamps, creative and bracelets, stickers made of embossed pieces, personalized glasses, blackboards, and mugs cut out images or letters for scrapbooking, and so on many more.

What Can You Do With Cricut

Create stickers that you can place on your car in your preferred objects

Create your own stencils that you can use to paint

* Create custom labels

You can personalize your pillows, shirts tablecloths, sweatshirts

* Make an endless array of Christmas decorations

You can personalize the glasses as well as the mugs

* Engrave the glass

* Create yourself your own wall stickers

* Make shapes using balsa or linden wood

* Create decals

* DIY slates

* Banner for the party

* Birthday invitations

* Sewing projects

* Scrapbooking templates with shapes

* Leather products (diaries or bracelets.)

* Puzzle

There are a variety of models and the features included with each model differ from one model to the next. But there are certain items that are universally available with the machines.

Every machine comes with:

* Cricut cutter

• One blade with a fine tip, and One premium blade.

* A 12x12 inches "LightGrip" cutting mat.

The USB Cable

* A power adapter

A helpful guide to easy installation

* A trial membership for free for Cricut Access

- Access to over 25 completely free projects, ready to go

Materials needed for a practice project.

Certain models have additional components, like cutting wheels, different types of blades or a specific pen to write with.

Cricut Machine Cricut Machine is a plotter that is able to cut various materials, and draw or write on them. It could as well perforate them (create the tear lines that are typical of tickets to the cinema in a way) or engraving them (for instance Plexiglas as well as aluminum) and make reliefs (such as those in the case of embossingeven though at home it's actually it's a debossing) or fold lines (very beneficial if you are making boxes, tickets, cards or boxes, etc.). The machine can do one or the other , based on the tool (blade or tip) which we're employing. This will be one of the Rolls Royce of cutting machines. It's not without reason! Imagine any medium with a thickness of 3mm and the machine can cut it with the same power than the Cricut Explore as well as its rivals. What attracted me to this machine was that it has the capability of cutting and stamping leather. The Cricut machine is able to cut balsa, cardboard burlap, vinyl, flex (!)... and FABRIC. Yes! That's right! Not only cotton! There are many kinds of fabrics can be found! The Design Space you can find various kinds of fabrics like silk, jersey, velvet and lacing! The Maker cuts about 100 different types of materials that are that are up to 3mm thick. Another great feature of the Maker is that you can write on it!

Whatever kind of material we wish to use for the maker (paper wood, jeans, etc.) ...), we'll have to insert it into the machine following the process of making it adhere to specially reusable mats , mats equipped with a less or more durable layer of glue If we're using paper, we'll use mats that have the layer of a less resilient glue. However, if you are using wood, then we'll choose an adhesive mat that has a more robust coating of adhesive. The Cricut machine comes with a dual carriage that allows two tasks to be accomplished with a single stroke. This means that it is feasible to create drawings (or utilize"scoring tool "scoring tool "to create folds) and cut simultaneously.

Cartridge

Designs are created using components stored on cartridges. Each cartridge comes with an overlay for the console and a booklet. The overlay on the console is plastic and shows the most important features of that cartridge, as it were. However, as of late Provo Craft has discharged an "All-inclusive overlay" which is compatible for all cartridges released from August 1st 2013. The purpose behind this all-inclusive overlay was to ease cutting by merely learning one console overlay instead of learning the overlays for each individual cartridge. Designs can be deleted on an PC using the Cricut Design Studio programming, using an USB connected Gypsy device, or be properly inputted onto the Cricut machine using the overlay for the console. There are two types of cartridges, shape and textual. Each cartridge is equipped with a range of creative highlights that can consider a variety of cuts that are available from a single cartridge. As of today, there are around 275 cartridges available (independently by the computer) and include texts and forms as well as new cartridges added every month. Each cartridge works with Cricut's programming and are required to be registered with an individual client and aren't able to be given away or sold. Cartridges purchased to be used on a machine that is suspended is likely to end in futility when the machine has been shut down. Cricut has the authority required to end support for specific versions of their products at any time they want, which may result in making certain cartridges rapidly obsolete.

Cricut Craft Room is a Cricut Craft Room programming empowers users to join images from different cartridges, merge pictures, and stretch/turn images but it does not make use of the possibility of the creation of designs that are not based on a particular design. The program also allows the user to view the images on the screen prior to beginning cutting, so that the finished product can be observed prior to the cutting process. As a result of Adobe's withdrawal in the matter of Flash, Cricut declared it was closing Cricut Craft Room at 15 July 2018. Cricut customers who have "heritage" devices were given discounts to refresh models that work using

Cricut Design Space. Beginning on July 16, 2018 Design Space is the primary program that can be used to create projects. Design Space isn't perfect with cartridges that were previously purchased to use with Cricut Mini. Cricut Mini, which was powered by nightfall in the month of October, 2018.

Third-party

Provo Craft has been effectively incompatible with the use of programming tools from outsiders which could allow Cricut owners to take out designs and use the device without relying on the exclusive cartridges. A similar review of the bite-the-dust cutting machines, the site TopTenReviews discovered that the Cricut is "restricted to cutting only designs cut from several cartridges" as one of the main drawbacks of the Cricut machine but the review found that this could be a common occurrence for certain. Two programs that were in the past, be used to create and then acquire Cricut machines to eliminate personal designs (utilizing such tools as self-assertive TrueType styles for text or SVG group images) were the Make-the-Cut (MTC) along with Craft Edge's Sure Cuts A Lot (SCAL). In April 2010, Provo Craft opened a lawful action against the makers of Make-the-Cut and then in January of 2011, it brought a suit against Craft Edge to stop the transfer for the SCALE application. In both cases the distributors negotiated in a settlement with Provo Craft and expelled support for Cricut from their products. These projects are accessible alongside various other cutters for home use. Based on the contents of its legal complaint at Craft Edge, "Provo Craft uses a variety of methods to obscure and encode its USB connections between Cricut DesignStudio [a design application that is included in the hardware] and Cricut e-shaperin order to safeguard Provo Craft's restrictive software and firmware, and to prevent attempts to record cuts commands". Provo Craft battled that so as to understand and mimic this darkened standard, Craft Edge had dismantled the DesignStudio program, in violation to the terms of the End User License Agreement, in this manner (the organization confirmed) violating copyright laws. Provo Craft additionally affirmed that Craft Edge were damaging its trademark "Cricut" in a statement that the product would be used alongside Cricut machines. Provo Craft declared this was likely "to cause confusion, miscalculation, or double handling in relation to the source or the starting point of the product or benefits, and wassusceptible to misrepresent an association, sponsorship or permit to the products or ventures of Defendant to Provo Craft. "The result of this is those who own more mature versions of Cricut devices that were "power-dark" through the cutting off programming support, are not able to elective programs for their obsolete machines.

Materials That Can Be Use In A Cricut Machine

There are numerous different materials that machines can utilize for any project that you want to do and we'll break down which machines will work with which materials. The thing to remember is there's certain materials which the machine can cut that other machines are unable to cut. There are more than 100 different kinds of fabrics are cut are cut by the maker, in fact. The official website of Cricut machines is updated regularly in the types of fabrics the machines are able to cut, therefore, you should visit their website because of this. When you do this you will be able to see the things you are still able to cut, and what might have been removed from the list.

Explore series only cut certain objects, and we'll go over them right now.

Explore series Explore series can cut these things:

* Tattoo paper

* Washi tape

* Paint chips

* Wax paper

* Faux suede

* Wrapping paper

* Washi paper

* Poster board

* Parchment paper

* Sticker paper

* Construction paper

* Photo paper

* Print fabric

* Magnetic sheets

* Bags for grocery shopping made of paper

* Craft foam

* Window vinyl with a cling

* Cardstock

* Flannel

* Vellum

* Duck cloth

* Wool felt

* Cork board

* Tissue paper

* Duct tape

* Matte vinyl

* Vinyl with iron-on

* Leather that is up to 2.0 millimeters thick

* Sheet duct tape

* Oil cloth

* Soda cans

* Stencil film

* Glitter foam

* Metallic vellum

* Burlap

* Transparency film

* Chipboard up to 2.0 millimeters thick

* Aluminum metal up to .14 millimeters thick

* Stencil vinyl

* Glitter vinyl

* Glossy vinyl

* Faux leathers up to 1.0 millimeter thick

Fabrics that are used in Explore series, when used with Explore series, should be stabilized using Heat N Bond. Some examples of fabrics are listed in the list below:

* Denim

* Felt

* Silk

* Polyester

Other things to be cut by can be cut by the Explore Series can cut will be described below:

* Chalkboard vinyl

* Adhesive vinyl

* Aluminum foil

* Cardboard

* Stencil film

* Dry erase vinyl

* Vinyl that can be printed

* Outdoor vinyl

* Wood birch as thick as .5 millimeters thick

* Cardboard with corrugated edges

* Shrink plastic

* Metallic vellum

* White core

* Rice paper

* Mat for framing photos

* Pearl cardstock

* Cereal boxes

* Freezer paper

* Iron-on

* Printable iron-on

* Glitter iron-on

* Foil iron-on

* Foil embossed papers

* Neon iron-on

* Matte iron-on

The Maker is able to cut anything that Explore series Explore series is able to cut, however it is able to cut much more, as the Explore series has three blades, while the Maker is equipped with six. Because they have six blades means that it's able to cut more fabric and more thick fabrics as well. It is also different in comparison to the Explore series in that the Maker does not require Heat N Bond to stabilize fabric. This is great since it means you can visit an online fabric shop and pick the fabric you want to use to create a project without preparation , and without any additional materials.

The Maker can also be able to make use of the rotary blade, too. This kind of blade is brand new and differs from other blades that Explore machines utilize because it spins, and it also twists in an gliding and rolling motion. The rolling motion is designed allow the maker to cut from both sides as well as upwards and downwards. The ability of a blade to cut in any direction is sure aid you in the ability to create amazing projects. The Maker can even be used cutting (up at) up to three layers cotton light simultaneously. This is ideal for projects that require cut-offs that are uniform.

The Maker also has the ability to utilize the knife blade, which is more precise and is more efficient than previous models before it. The knife blade can make cuts up to 2.4 millimeters. This blade can also use 10 times more power to cut than other machines and also.

That being said the Maker has the ability to cut over 100 different fabrics that other machines cannot. We'll be providing the names of some of these fabrics below:

* Waffle cloth

* Jacquard

* Gossamer

* Khaki

* Damask
* Faille
* Heather
* Lycra
* Mesh
* Calico
* Crepe paper
* Gauze
* Interlock knit
* Grocery bag
* Acetate
* Chantilly lacing
* Boucle
* Corduroy
* EVA foam
* Tweed
* Tulle

* Moleskin

* Fleece

* Jersey

* Muslin

* Jute

* Terry cloth

* Velvet

* Knits

* Muslin

Keep in mind that this is only getting a glimpse of the possibilities that the Maker is able to cut. There are plenty more, as the Maker is thought to be the most powerful machine, and is the most powerful among the four. It is excellent for sewing, and there are a myriad of projects available on Design Space. A machine that can accessibility to the projects, and the ability to cut larger materials, means you have the ability to take your craft skills to a new level.

Chapter 2: How To Set-Up The Cricut Maker Machine

Setup Up the Machine

In the beginning, you'll need to set up your Cricut machine. In the beginning, you'll need to set up a space. The craft space is a great location, but If you're not sure of where you can put it, I'd suggest installing it in a dining area If you can. You should have a power outlet near by or an extension cord that is reliable.

After that, go through the instruction. Most of the time, you can just immediately begin working with the machine, but when it comes to Cricut equipment, this could be quite laborious. The best way to get started is read through all items you receive along with your machine. Although we'll cover the set-up in this guide If you're not sure then take a look in the manual.

Be sure to have plenty of space surrounding the machine, since mats will be loaded in and out and will require that tiny bit of space to move around.

The next thing you need to create is, of course, the machine that will be where the designs are made. It is essential that whatever device you're using is connected to the internet because you'll be required for downloading Cricut Design Space. Cricut Design Space app. If the machine is older then the Explore Air 2, it is required to be connected into directly. If it's a device that is wireless, similar to Air 2 Air 2, you can simply connect it to your computer and from there, create the things you'll need to create.

Once you've got your Cricut first installed, you'll want to master the use of Design Space.

Utilizing Cricut Software

That's right, Cricut machines use a software known as Cricut Design Spaces which is why you'll need to ensure you've downloaded it and installed before you can start. Download the app if you plan to use a smartphone or tablet, or if you're on the computer, go to http://design.cricut.com/setup to get the software. If your device isn't connected before, ensure that you have Bluetooth compatible on your device, or that the cord is connected. To turn on your Cricut press on the power button. After that, you'll go to settings, and you'll find your Cricut model listed in Bluetooth settings. Select that option, and from there the device will prompt to enter an Bluetooth passcode into it. Make it something simple and simple to remember.

After that You can then begin using Design Space.

If you're in online mode, there are numerous projects are available to use. To help you with this tutorial, I recommend that you select a simple one like"Enjoy Card," which is an "Enjoy Card" project that you can purchase by completing the automatic.

You've connected everything Let's get to the first cut of this project.

Transferring Cartridges and Keypad

The first cut you'll do involves keypad input and cartridges and they are typically done by using"Enjoy Card," the "Enjoy Card" project you receive immediately. When all is in place you can select the project and then you'll be able to use the tools and equipment included in the project.

It is necessary to configure the smart dial before you start with your project. It's located situated on the right hand edge of Explore Air 2, and it's the method you use to select the materials you'll use. Adjust the dial to the kind of material you'd like because this will assist in making sure you've got the proper blade settings. There are half settings available for those who are in between tasks.

For instance, suppose you have a light cardstock. You can select that setting or the half setting. After you have selected this setting inside Design Space, your machine will automatically adjust to the proper setting.

You can also select the fast mode. It is located in the "set, load go" area of the screen. You will be able to check the position of the box beneath the indicator for the dial's position. After that, press the button to create your cut. But, fast mode can be extremely noisy, so be aware.

We've already mentioned cartridges. Although they aren't commonly employed in Explore Air 2 machines anymore however, they are useful in beginning projects. To get them, after you've installed access to the Design Space software and everything is connected, open the hamburger menu, and you'll be able to select "ink cartridges." Click the Cricut button, and then, from there, select to use the Cricut device. The machine will tell you to insert your cartridge into. When it's found, it'll instruct you to connect the cartridge.

Remember, however that once you've linked the cartridge, you cannot make use of it on other machines The only restriction for these cartridges.

Once you've confirmed it After that, you can access images and then click on the cartridges option to select those you wish to build. You can sort the cartridges in order to find what you require as well as look through the images tab to find other cartridges you have either purchased or uploaded.

Digital cartridges are available that is, you purchase them on the internet and select the images from available choices. They're not physical, therefore there's no need for linking.

Loading and unloading Your Paper

For loading paper into the Cricut machine, you'll need to ensure that the paper measures at minimum three inches by three inches. If it's not, it won't cut efficiently. It is recommended to use normal paper to do this.

To complete this job, you'll have to place the sheet on the mat for cutting. It should be one which you need to use now and take off the film. Set a corner of your paper on the paper that you will be instructed to align the paper's corners. After that, place straight onto your cutting mat to ensure the proper adhesion. Once you've done this, you can put it in the machine and follow the directions. You'll need to ensure that you keep your paper in place in the paper. Make sure you press on the "load the paper" key you can notice as you go. If it isn't working the paper, you can press the key to unload the paper then try it again until you see it.

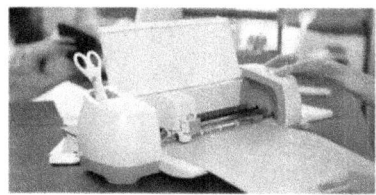

Before you begin any cutting on your design, make sure you always make a test cut in the same spot. A few people do not bother to do this, however it's extremely beneficial when learning how to operate the Cricut. If you don't, you'll be unable to have the right pressure in certain situations So, get in your routine to do it on your own pieces.

Chapter 3: Everything You Should Learn About Cricut Design Space

How do I download Cricut Design Space

is it design.cricut.com and you'll be required to sign in or create an account with a account and password. Sign up on the site and be sure to note down your login information to ensure that you don't need to log out again in the future. After you've taken care of that, simply click an option to create a new project at the top right corner of the screen. This will prompt that you need to download Design Space. Design Space plugin. After the download process is finished, you'll need opening the download file according to your browser or computer.

If you're using a Chrome browser, it will appear display on your download bar, located on the bottom. Select the tab to open, and then select run or next when you are asked.

Follow the prompts for downloading. You'll need to agree to these terms of service, then select install. The process is simple and the prompts will guide you through each step. In the end, Design Space is downloaded and you're now ready to begin exploring.

Before your machine is able to cut out designs You will need create your designs in Design Space (also called Design Space canvas).

When you are on the canvas utilize the menu to the left to start your designs.

* Click Upload to upload SVG images or files that you plan to cut. SVG is an abbreviation for Scalable Vector Graphic and it is the most commonly used cut-off file since it's clear. SVG files are available everywhere. You can find SVG files at websites, Etsy, and other sites.

The menu to the left the left side is Shapes. You can use circles, squares and stars and many other shapes to create your own designs. If you plan to score cards or work on other paper projects You'll find scoring lines in this article.

The third item in the menu on the left is text. There are numerous possibilities to work with text like curving text or creating monograms making your own fonts.

* The fourth option on this menu will be Images. When you click on the images icon, you'll be taken to the images available if are a subscriber to Cricut Access or the designs that you can purchase from Cricut in the absence of a subscription.

The fifth item in the menu on left is Projects. If you click on Projects there will be an overview of projects available for auction. But, there's a different dropdown menu you can select the projects you want to purchase. The saved projects are found in this area.

The sixth option in the menu on the left is Templates. Some craftspeople do not utilize this option, however you can make use of them to figure out the dimensions of the design you want to cut as well as the way it will appear on a shirt or an apron. Remember, this feature is an aid to design, and the actual design won't be cut.

The seventh option on the menu left is the button New+. If you are looking to begin an entirely new project then this is the button to hit. Always save your current project , if you plan to save it prior to starting another one. The save button is at the top of the right-hand corner.

Cricut Design Space Top Menu

To better understand Cricut Design Space, let's look at the menu on the top.

The menu on the top will only be available once you've got written out your text or have uploading a design. So, starting from the left side is an Undo button, which can be used to correct errors. The button to right is it's Redo button, which can be used to repeat the process.

The Deselect button comes next and serves in the same way as selecting. The Edit button follows and comes with an option dropdown menu consisting of copy, paste, and flip. The next button is the Size which you can click to alter the actual size of your design . You can also examine the lower right corner of the design to make use of the two-way directional Arrow.

The bottom left on the screen is an unlock button. It is comprised of an arrow that can be used in four directions to make designs wider without making them taller , or making them taller by expanding them.

The next option is the tool for rotation which allows designs to be rotated in every possible angle. The final feature of the menu's top is coordinates of x and y. These coordinates are that are used to set the design's position onto the paper.

How do I weld?

It's a intimidating for those who are a Cricut Space beginner to use the weld tool. However once you've become more proficient and confident, it will open the door to a variety of projects since it's an instrument that is frequently used.

The tool for welding is located in the lower left corner in Design Space, under the layers panel. The other tools near it include: contour, flatten and slice tools.

Within Cricut Design Space, the weld tool can be used to accomplish the following:

* connects cursive text with scrap to allow it to be cut as a single word , instead of letters

* Combine different shapes, layers, and layers into one layer image

* Cut lines of different shapes and then cut them into one large image

i. In order to be able to apply weld shapes or text, the shape or text you want to join should be overlapping or touching one another.

ii. Select the layer that you want to join; choose a layer, press 'ctrl' to select the next layer. After you have selected the two layers then click 'weld'. If you plan to join all the layers onto your canvas, select all to select all layers, and then click "weld"..

iii. If you glue multiple layers together, they will form an image in one and is split with one color on one mat.

If you do not select multiple layers, the welding option isn't accessible to use.

To weld text in order to weld text, you must ensure that all the letters are touching one another. Therefore, you must reduce the spacing between letters until they start to be in contact with each other. After that then you can choose everything and click to join.

How do I cut

This tool, called the slicer is an option of Cricut Design Space that cuts one design element from another. It can be used to cut text from a form or cut a form from another or cut shapes that overlap from one another. Here is an example where we cut out text from the heart shape.

i. Select a font

Choose any font you like however, you must reduce the spacing between letters to 0.9 to ensure that your letters link to each other.

ii. Apply the text

After you're finished with spacing, you need to change the letters into one image using the welding tool. If you glue the letters together, it permanently joins the design elements together into one single image.

iii. Select an SVG

There is an SVG of a heart from Lovesvg.com. It is necessary to separate everything , then simply remove the elements that are not needed.

iv. Choose the dimensions of your design

It is necessary to alter the size of the image. Based on the size you prefer, just enter the desired size in the"width" box. In this instance we'll use 5.5 inches.

V. Place the designs in a row.

It is necessary to place the wording and the heart by clicking on the 'arrange' button..

vi. Make use of the slice tool.

Once you've got your design correctly, choose your text , hold down the 'ctrl' keys then select the heart, and press'slice'. You can now remove all the content from your heart and erase.

vii. After you have completed your design you are now ready to cut the vinyl.

How to Flatten

The flatten tool can be that allows you to convert multiple layers of images into a single layer.

What is Flatten Do in Cricut Design Space?

By using the flatten tool you can accomplish the followingresults:

Cut lines should be removed from images.

* Convert multi-layered images to one image

* Used to transform regular images to printable ones to print and cut

* Used to preserve the distinctive colors of multi-layered photos.

Utilizing the flatten tool

Select the layers that you want to flatten and flatten, click'select all' or press the key 'ctrl' to select the layers

* Once you have selected to flatten, click the corner in the right-bottom

* Once you have done that the image will be flattened.

How do I attach

In essence, there are two main reasons to use the attach tool

* To make sure that you keep writing lines and scoring in the right spot

* To ensure that shapes are on the mat in the right place the mat, as they appear on the canvas

Use the Attach tool to keep the same arrangement

If you would like all parts of your project remain in the exact place while cutting, just in the same way as they appear on your CDS canvas you must:

* Choose all the items of each color

* Click "attach" at the lower left corner

Repeat the procedure with each layer of color until they're all nested beneath an label that reads "attach'

With the attach tool you'll be able to cut your projects exactly as you laid the Cricut canvas.

How do you group/ungroup?

Group in Cricut Design Space means to join several layers in one layer. In contrast, Ungroup means breaking up groups of layers into separate layers. There are various kinds of layers that are group-based, and If a layer has been grouped several times, you'll be required to ungroup them several times in order to fully separate them.

Group to group: To create a group, you will need to select the layers that you want to group by using the mouse and then moving it over the design. You can also select different layers from the layer panel with an keyboard shortcut. To select more layers, you need to use the 'ctrl' key and select the layers from your desktop. After selecting, you need to right-click your mouse and then press on the group button. If you want to, you can also select an option to create several groups within groups because it is easier to manage complicated designs.

The way you work in Design Space, groups work more efficiently with layers, particularly when you're trying to alter the design in a particular area. With Group you are able to easily expand or shrink the choice.

Ungroup: It's easy to remove designs that are grouping together. To remove a group, you have select the layer that you want to remove and then right-click your mouse and then select Ungroup. Ungroup button or Ungroup. The layers may be grouped several times. Therefore, if you plan to completely Ungroup then you must repeatedly select the layer and click Ungroup until you're completely completed.

The principal reason for using this Ungroup function is the ability to modify or modify a particular aspect of the design. The alteration could be physical or manipulating a portion of a design through welding, attaching or by other means that do not touch the remainder parts of the plan.

How to duplicate/delete

If you plan to duplicate the layer or set layers, select the portion of the design layers you wish to duplicate. Right click on your mouse and then select the Duplicate button.

However If you plan to erase a single layer or set of layers will need to choose the portion of the design or layers you wish to remove by right-clicking your mouse, then select the delete button.

If you have two designs , and you plan to keep only one, choose the design you want to delete, click on your mouse and then select the delete option.

Utilizing Text using Text Cricut Design Space

After you have signed in to Cricut Design Space, select one of the three locations that are marked with arrows, to begin an entirely new project. Click the three line icon in the upper left side to go to "New Project". When you begin your new project, you'll be directed to a grid design space, also known as Canvas. Canvas. Click on the left sidebar, which includes the icon for text. A small box will appear with an additional arrow, within which you are able to type in your text. Once you've entered the text choose a font that is at the bottom left of the of the arrow.

Starting by Text

Begin typing your message by clicking the icon for text on the toolbar left. Text boxes will open within which you can begin typing your text. The font, style and size as well as the spacing between letters and lines are available by clicking to the toolbar at the top. It is recommended to write your text first, and then modify it in the following step.

Fonts

The option 'Font' will show a range of fonts available. You can view only your own fonts by clicking the system or view those offered through Cricut fonts by pressing Cricut. If you've got a favorite font, make use of the search function.

You also can choose to narrow the fonts in case you're looking for a multilayer or writing font.

How to add your own fonts

If you'd rather include your own Fonts there are several sites readily available, like CreativeMarket.com, TheHungryJpeg.com or DaFont.com with a huge choice of fonts to choose from. Additionally, DesignBundles.net provides creative bundles for purchase with designs and fonts that come with commercial licenses so that you are able to sell them on any risk. Making your own products to sell requires the Font is licensed commercially. license. Once you have chosen the Font you would like to work with, locate that file in your system, and then open it. Since Fonts are in a zip-file, you must open the extract file that is likely to be opened automatically. After the files have been extracted are opened, the different versions from those of the Font will be shown as 'Original Bold and 'Italics'. It is not required to install all variations, as the 'Original' font can modify within your design software. There are two variants known as 'Open Type Font True Type Font are offered. Their installation is contingent on the features on the system you're using. Therefore, you should try both. After the file you'd like is chosen, right click on it, and then install. The new Font selected will be listed under the heading 'System Fonts within the Design Space. While you're installing the new Font it is advised to close the design space, then restart it to see the new Font.

How do I access special characters?

You can get access to special characters with Humble Scrip which provides many choices. It is accessible by typing "character map" in the search box of your system. The app will show up. A drop-down menu will show the font you're working with. Select the Advanced View option to ensure that the option which is correctly selected. Modify the Character changed to Unicode and then group according to the Unicode Subrange. In this step the new box will be displayed to display this Unicode Subrange. Scroll all the way to the bottom , and then select "Private use of Characters'.

Regarding your design location when you're looking to remove a letter from the text box and want it replaced, simply press control followed by the "V" key at the same time, to paste the new letter. The design will appear as it's a square, however the text will alter. If you want to alter the size of your text, select the font size in the upper toolbar. When you are happy with the final outcome regarding the size as well as spacing, you can highlight the text and choose. Click the align button in the toolbar at the top. If you want you could align your text to the left or center it, or even align with the correct direction.

How do you Curve Text

Curving text is quite easy to achieve in the design space, since it's essentially of sliding the text towards the left. When you do this your text will start to be curving upwards. Once you have done this it is possible to use the option to space letters if you require adjustments. In the end, you'll be able to select all of the options and then place your lines in the center.

How to Create the Stencil

Perfect for hand-painted signs, stencils with designs space can be designed using the shapes tool in the left side of the toolbar. After pressing the unlock button at the bottom left you can stretch your design into the shape of a rectangle. Add the text you wish to include onto your stencil, using or without the guidelines mentioned previously in relation to spacing, centering and sizing, curvings, or fonts. When you are happy with the result Highlight and select all the text, then hit the attach button in the right side of the toolbar. Choose both text as well as the box, then select the align tool from the toolbar at the top.

How to Use Contour with Text

Contour can be used to eliminate or cover up unwanted parts of an image or design. For using this tool you need choose the layer or image (one at each) you wish to edit and then click to use the tool near the bottom in the layer panel.

As a default, it's not possible to use the contour tool with text. One reason is the fact that text is dependent on the font. This means that the program will not allow any modification that is too extreme to contour.

You must join your text to the weld before you can utilize the contour feature. for this, simply choose the word or text you want to use and then click the welding button on the lower right on the Panel of Layers. After welding it, you'll be able shape your text or word and remove the blank spaces or letters you're planning to eliminate.

Be sure that you save copies your text in case you plan to utilize it in the future because once you've welded it and then you'll be unable to modify it later.

How to Edit Images in Cricut Design Space With The Slice Tool

It is possible to use this Slice Tool to modify images using Cricut Design Space. To edit images, follow these steps. are the steps you need to follow;

Upload your image to your canvas using Cricut Design Space. For this to be done, simply click on the image, then click on the insert image button.

The program lets users upload multiple images at a given time to the canvas.

To begin working on your design, you must to increase the size of your image by clicking on the bottom corner , then moving it down. Make sure you clearly see all the parts within the photo.

If there's any area of the image that you'd like to eliminate You can employ Slice Tool to remove it. On the toolbox to the left click on Shapes and then click on the square.

You can click on the left-bottom circle below the square to open it. If you see an icon for locking Click it. After that you've unlocked the square. This means you can change it into any shape you'd like using the right-bottom circle. The square can be used to substitute the missing portion in the picture.

* With the area highlighted, hold and press your shift key. Click the bubble image using your mouse. This action will highlight both.

* If you have both the image as well as the square highlighted make use of your mouse to use the slice tool located at the lower right corner.

* Remove the pieces from your slice and remove them any you'd like to.

Continue with the process until you are able to successfully modify the image.

Chapter 4: What Can I Do With Cricut Machine?

What is a Cricut?

The ricut machines are growing in popularity in the craft world because they don't have cartridges as they did with the earlier machines, since everything is digital. It allows you to design and create fonts as large as you like as long as they are stored on your computer. These computers have advanced capabilities, which means that they are able to work with Bluetooth or Wi-Fi. This means that you are able to design using your iPhone or laptop computer or even your iPad This makes it possible to create directly from your iPad or your iPhone or computer or your computer, depending on your preference.

One of the great advantages of Cricut machines is that you can use them for anything, since there are a myriad of options of projects and materials that you can make use of. The Cricut machine is believed to be a die-cutting device. In some ways, they're often compared to printers. Printers print the design you've designed using your computer. An Cricut however, can cut the design using whatever material you choose to make use of. It can be used as an printer. If you opt to use it you will find an accessory slot inside the machine that you will need to insert markers. The computer draw the pattern on your behalf and give your designs a lovely handwritten appearance.

Every machine has its own method to cut things which means that you'll be able to see this with the particular machine you choose. It is possible to cut different materials to make various items, such as leather for bracelets made of leather. This machine is designed for precise cuts. They are able to cut more than a hundred different materials. The Maker machine, the fourth machine we'll be discussing can cut everything that the other machines could do, as well as over 100 other materials too, particularly fabrics.

Every machine has its own method to cut things and you'll notice this based on the machine you purchase. It is possible to make a variety of items using them too. Cut fun shapes to use for scrapbooking. This is regarded as to be a lost art form or an activity for the older generation however it's a lot of fun and an excellent way of conserving memories. It is possible to design T-shirts rubber bracelets and car stickers or even envelopes. There are endless options to choose from and all are enjoyable and can be used as business solutions for those who want to be more creative when you create custom designs.

This machine is perfect for cutting precise pieces of paper, however, it is crucial to understand that, although the paper is just one of the many things it is able to cut, it's not the only thing it can cut. It has the ability to cut more, something we'll explore in a future chapter. They also have the ability to score material making folding quick and precise, giving an elegant look and they can also draw and write using pencils.

The Cricut machine comes with an application which allows you to create your own designs and upload images. Through the application, you can import your cuts and also purchase designs. It's easy to use and people have found it to be a wonderful option utilize the machine to its greatest capacity.

The machines have been in use for some time and the majority of work was previously done using cartridges. If you have an older Cricut cartridge, you'll be able to utilize it with the new machine, and your files will be in good condition and accessible for use. Since it's now done digitally, if not own a cartridge, you'll get access to an extensive collection of cutting files. In addition to the plethora of things it can do also, it can engrave well. Engraving is an enticing craft desire right now, and as such, a lot of people are rushing to master it and use it to their advantage.

But, there are a few cautions to be aware of when purchasing Cricut machines. The majority of people recommend you purchase it through the site itself instead of any third-party, specifically from the most popular stores on the internet. Today, many craft stores, like Hobby Lobby or Joann are secure retailers and you'll get exactly what you're buying. There are some disadvantages when buying from these stores, too. Prices are usually higher than the prices you see at the Original Equipment Manufacturer (OEM) website, and you can use coupons on all Cricut Cricut products. Additionally there is no way to get a bundle deal that can save you lots of money as well as provide other tools you require.

Another retailer that is popular is Amazon. The majority of crafters purchase their cutting equipment directly via the site. But, since there have been issues with Amazon and its customers, it's becoming more risky to purchase larger purchases through Amazon While you are covered by their returns policy, this will not protect you from the stress of dealing with orders that went wrong. Amazon's prices are cheaper but you'll usually discover that they are prices are only a couple of dollars more. If you choose to purchase from Amazon be sure to be sure to follow these guidelines that you must be extremely cautious prior to placing your order. Also, make sure you purchase the latest model. If you purchase a specific model, you're trying to find matches for the model you are looking for however, it might be different. Don't just glance at the image. You must read the description as well as everything which is described. Make sure you know the brand of the various accessories and also check the brand of everything that is included. It could not be worth it If those extras you get for free aren't of the standard and of the name, you're looking for the item to have. If you are using inferior materials and products, you'll end up with inferior projects in the end. This is why you must stay clear of this.

Cricut has been a major hit in the world of Cricut There are many advantages to owning one of the machines. Cricut's Explore Maker and Maker are both extremely flexible; many applications used for blogs or social media originate out of one of these machines. Many people use it to create projects that do not will see daylight However, many people also utilize it for projects that they utilize in their daily lives. There are many more ideas to inspire you to create every day that shows the fantastic opportunity this machine could offer you. Many people know and recognize crafting, even though crafters make many projects that don't see the sunlight up in the morning, they produce the same kinds of projects as those who do. And with the option to save this machine provides it is possible to return to your projects later to improve the ones you've completed before completing the project. This is a fantastic alternative when a holiday is coming close and you do not have any gifts or some last-minute events approaching and you're looking for innovative ideas to bring to the event. The projects that are available made with this tool are compact and quick to complete and therefore don't take a long time to complete and don't need numerous resources. This is a fantastic alternative if you're an active person and don't have a lot of time to make crafts but nevertheless want to do something exciting to make.

Furthermore the other benefit of purchasing the Cricut tool is that it can help you save time. This is especially relevant if you're experienced with hand cutting. The machine will do it faster and also saves you from throwing up, and the frustration of having to deal with. You can complete tasks which you've never considered doing because there's no way you could do these intricate cuts manually. The possibility of creating custom-designed projects is a huge advantage, as it is possible to upload design as well as images. Every project you create can be customized precisely how you would like it or want the item to appear. It is also possible to personalize gifts as well. One of the most appealing benefits users have mentioned is that it's simple to master. It is possible to feel overwhelmed by the technology due to the fact that they have lots of options, however it's easy to learn how to utilize Design Space, because it is easy to use and user-friendly. There is a wide variety of create-it-now projects with an simple to learn curve.

There are more complex tasks you can accomplish using these machines, however there are plenty of tutorials on the internet , as and books similar to this one to aid you in understanding how to use the machine and manage more complex projects. Because this book is an introduction guide to these machines, we've included basic projects at the end of the book because you won't be able to tackle a more complex project at this point. However, the projects that are listed at the close of the book are difficult enough to provide you with some new information as well as give you an experience in cutting.

The Cricut creates projects with greater precision and looks more professional. Also, it helps you avoid hassles since you won't waste the same amount of material. Additionally, it's much faster than hand-crafting and you can save time. Many who have been hand-crafting all their lives know the value of this machine. They know that they are not just saving time, but you're also preventing yourself from unnecessary discomfort that could cause long-term issues later throughout your life.

There are certain instances that you should delay purchasing the Cricut in case you don't have the desire to become maker, and think you could just purchase items from an online store instead of making it by yourself, then you will not be using your Cricut. It isn't the case for all, but it could be applied to certain. It is necessary to have a motivation to create things by yourself in order to utilize this machine. If you don't want to make anything by yourself is the case, you won't utilize the machine to its full potential. It'll just remain in storage unattended.

If you only desire to purchase things simply just because they look cool, this is likely be difficult for you, too. People buy things simply just because they look cool however, they don't utilize them. You will end up buying a device as well as the tools and products to go along with it. However, If you purchase it simply because it looks cool and you like it, then you may not use it. If you are looking for something that is cool, it can be expensive , especially with the equipment that it comes with. If this is the case rather than spending money on something you'll never use, spend the money on something you'll. If you think this is cool and you are enticed to build things by yourself it could be the perfect machine to purchase for yourself. What we're saying is to be honest about yourself. If you are awestruck by the concept of this device, but you're sure that you're never going to get it from the package and actually use that machine then it isn't the right machine for you. But, if you're certain that this machine is among the most amazing items you've ever seen and you can't wait to try it out or discover what it can accomplish then this could be a great purchase.

Therefore, don't just take a look at the image for the sole purpose. It is important to read the description as well as everything that is listed in the advertisement you are viewing. It is also important to make sure you know the names of all the accessories and verify the manufacturer of everything you will receive with the new machine. The offer may not be as appealing as you believe it to be in the event that the accessories which are offered aren't of good quality and come from a company which is recognized. If you are using inferior materials that aren't of the highest quality, you're going to end up with projects that aren't the best in terms of results. This is the reason you should choose an item of high-end quality and high quality equipment and other accessories.

After we've provided you with some details about Cricut machines overall. Let's be more specific and talk about the specific machine. The first machine we'll look at is part of the Explore series. The Explore series comprises three machines that are part of the series. It includes three models: the Explore One, the Explore Air as well as Explore Air 2. Explore Air 2; the latter is the most well-known among the three. The Explore series is gaining popularity because of its vibrant colors, as well as the advantages it provides. Its Air 2 is available in 12 colors, meaning that users can be content with the fact that they've chosen a product that stands apart.

Explore One Explore One is the most basic of the cutters within the line. This means that it will be the cheapest among the three. It is the best choice for anyone who doesn't want to make too much. It can score and write on, as well as cut a variety of materials. It also has a fine-point blade that cuts crafts materials. It also works with the deep-point blade as well as it comes with a scoring device. The company defines this as a "starter" machine. It can also contain materials for a test project.

In the chapter, we explain on tips, the reasons this is crucial and how you can make use of it. When you purchase this Cricut machine on the Cricut site, you'll get the accessories included along with the machine.

Explore Air Explore Air can be described as the very first Air model designed specifically for this series. Due to the popularity it received it was followed by the launch Air 2 Air 2 shortly afterwards. Similar to its predecessor the Explore One, it can score, cut and write on a hundred materials, and comes with a fine-point blade. It's also compatible with other blades we've mentioned. The machine boasts that its performance matches value. It works with materials like glitter papers and fabrics that allow you to make many different designs. It includes a double-tool holder and Bluetooth wireless technology.

The last model in the line is called the Explore Air 2. This is the top of the three and it comes with the greatest features. It offers a wide range of options of the things you can do along with it, and you can bundle the machine with other machines. The machine is twice as efficient than the one that came before it. It cuts through a hundred different materials, including specialty materials and is simple but high-quality. It works with other blades, similar to other models, and comes with bluetooth wireless technology. It is able to operate in Fast mode which means it can be used with well-known materials and will save time.

There are two options available when it comes to bundling. You can pick either an Essentials bundle as well as the everything bundle. This is crucial. The bundles come with the equipment as well as the features we've previously mentioned, that the Explore Air 2 includes. The Essentials bundle is normally priced at $418 . However, when it is on sale, it sells for just $270.

The Essentials bundle comes with the following products:

* Window clings in black

* The tool set that is the basic

Machine mat assortment pack (12 12")

* The blade is deep-point and comes with the housing that goes along with it

* The stylus for scoring

* A pen set (in Candy Shop)

One thing to remember about bundles it is that the items included in the bundle are able to be replaced according to availability. This is the case for the Everything bundle too.

The bundle typically sells for $588, however when it goes on sale it's reduced to $310. Since this bundle comes that includes everything, this will definitely include additional. The bundle comprised of the following items:

* Window clings in black

* Window clings in red

* The tool set that is the basic

* The stylus for scoring

* The blade that is deep-point and the housing it requires

* A set of pens (in wildflowers)

* Vinyl that can be printed

* Washi sheets (in designer)

* Transfer tape

* Poster Board (in metallic)

* Dry erase vinyl

* The pen set with the variety (in black)

The finest replacement fine-point blade

* Machine mat Variety pack (12 12")

• Faux-leather sampler (pebbled sampler with patina)

* Printable magnet sheets

* Trimmer for portable

* Vinyl sampler (in home)

* Printable sticker paper

* Printable iron-on (in dark)

The Maker is a series all by itself and has more capabilities and abilities than these machines in addition to the ability to cut more things. It has blades the other machines don't and is considered the best machine. If you're an individual who enjoys crafting or has lots of ideas to create then this will be the one you'll want for yourself. This is the top of four. Users have affirmed that it is top-quality at a reasonable price.

There are a variety of reasons people think this is most efficient tool, and it's worth the cost. It is possible to cut a variety of items (which we've talked about) It also gives you even more possibilities to create various projects since it can be used with heavier-duty materials. It's amazing when it comes to sewing, and it gives you the chance to make something unique and original. It also provides a more accurate and flawless cutting as it's outfitted with sharp knives. This means it can be done with greater grace and accuracy.

Another benefit of having the Maker instead of the other model is the capability to cut non-bonded fabric, meaning it doesn't need an stabilizer as do the machines of the Explore series. The Maker was developed to keep the future of crafting in the back of its mind. The company is already working on putting additional tools over the next few years that will work with the Maker. It's also a solid piece of equipment that is extremely robust. This means you need not be concerned about your product being damaged, as it's not likely to.

Because Design Space being so user-friendly and accessible to everyone, even the elderly will be able to utilize it and not experience problems with it. It is the same for beginning crafters and students. Another aspect that separates these machines from other models, manufactured by other companies within the same class is that they provide advantages that others have not. These machines are great for people who love creating patterns and can provide numerous ideas for new projects you can make thanks to the application.

The Cricut machines can also provide an accurate and professional appearance. If you're giving gifts to someone else, it looks incredible, and if you create items for your business the look stunning. Professionals know that your products need to appear professional. If you want your products to appear professional and look professional, this machine will help you achieve this. The Maker is superior to the other machines. The Maker is equipped with the rotary blade needed to cut fabrics for sewing projects, and it does not require backing material. The machine is able to cut more than three hundred materials . It is equipped with an adaptable tool system that delivers cutting efficiency at a professional level and also expandability. It comes with bluetooth wireless technology. It has the ability to use Fast mode which can provide speeds of upto two times quicker writing speed and cutting, resulting in better efficiency and efficiency in time.

Chapter 5: How To Create A Business In Cricut?

What Should You Think About When Thinking about Cricut's Profits from Business

It's because it's apparent that when selling crafts, the more small crafting, the more worth it is. A lower delivery fee, and less material, all of it is worth it.

The main thing I consider when putting together this list is the cost of materials, modern length and delivery issues as well as the possibility of attempting (because time is money!) and the credibility.

Materials cost. The cost of materials typically will be reflected in the pricing, However, you should not overlook the overhead expenses. Most of your money should spend the most of the budget, and purchase materials first. Additionally, there are likely to be leftover scraps and cloth when you buy in the bulk. It's possible to buy only the amount of cloth however it's never completely designed.

Shipping. For the seller it is usually possible by incorporating cost of shipping into the price. This is a good option if you're dealing with an expensive point object, however when the base price of the item is $5 and the shipping is $50, it isn't a good idea for the client who is already in the business.

Effort. If you want to see the most crafters promote their items, it's typically hard work and the love of. However, it can take off the joy, as making your own crafts for orders is a major part of your day. It's just something you need to think about. If you're selling a really complex vinyl piece Do you really need to spend an hour weeding it and then sell your work for just five dollars?

How to Turn Creativity into An Actual Business

You've become a professional crafter thanks to the creative designs of various Cricut cartridges. Your creative scrapbooking is the topic of conversation with your fellow Cricut users. Your amazing, custom-designed welcome card collections were the product of your creative Cricut designs. Companions disclose to you that your creation can contend with any financially-delivered welcome cards, or scrapbooks sold in your neighborhood stationery shop.

In the end, have you ever thought of making money out of your stunning and original art work? These are amazing strategies to earn money doing what you love.

Although a lot of people who craft appreciate their Cricut cutting machines however, they haven't achieved success with the device, and it doesn't perform in the way the way they think it will. Take advantage of this opportunity to provide your services to accept custom orders, and cut out records that customers are able to use. Art gatherings are a great opportunity to discover what others are looking for and then create the cut records and then sell them on the internet specifically on eBay.

Display your specially designed cards and invitations in local exhibitions and art stores. You can also provide them to their customers. A lot of people cannot imagine anything better than the opportunity to create a personalized card or message designed for special occasions like dedications, birthdays, commemorations or other events. Your design can be endless and distinctive because of the endless Cricut ideas.

There are always themed birthday parties for kids. Guardians love to celebrate their child's birthday by presenting them with themes such as an Disney costume party or the Pokemon party. It is possible to, with a bit of a problem, make some money by making accessories bundles for these occasions. Make and cut several of different themes that are stylistically appealing and make altered IDs or playing cards that children can share and trade with one another at the end of the event.

As scrapbooks become more and more popular with every passing day, using this Cricut machine to make cutting of pages for scrapbooks is a great way to sell to people who are avid about scrapbooks. As passionate as you are about scrapbooking, you'll have many plans and concepts.

Did you know that you could also offer your creative ideas to mortgage-holders or interior decorators who are passionate about the home? You can promote your profitable plans to local stores, or paint and backdrop stores, and hand them your flyers or business cards that promote your custom dividers and workmanship management.

Interior decorators may also purchase your services if you provide them with your customized home-designing projects. Your decals for dividers could consist made of any form, design or animation design you have created using Design Studio and vinyl sheets.

With your endless Cricut ideas, you could draw on your expertise and skills to earn additional income using Cricut technology and development and also continue your passion and hobby of creating stunning artwork that everyone can enjoy for many years.

Tips to make a Passionate Profit

Find out how to trust And Follow Your Senses

If you inquire of any successful businessperson what is the reason for their success at some point, they'll frequently mention it. It's not a costly educational or business degree they attended. For the most part, they affirm that one of the most important factors to success in business is trusting in your instincts. Success can be achieved by simply acting normally.

Consider a Coach

Business mentors are very popular in the present. Think about negotiating a deal with a professional mentor in scrapbooking who is knowledgeable of the business and the particular kind of energy-based scrapbook that couples are known to. Mentors can assist you in sharing the business skills and go around as a great guide to help you achieve your goals.

Showcase Your Talent with A Business Card for Artists

The downturn in the economy has left a lot of us feeling squeezed. Many people are looking for ways to save money throughout their lives. However there are instances where a purchase must be made, and careful research is often the basis of the leadership process. If you own their own company they face these circumstances, which is why it is possible to compare with the past to make your business be noticed. If you're involved in the craft industry an excellent method to connect with potential customers is by distributing an artist's business card.

Give the Quality of Your Work A Chance Shine Through

A professional business card is your gateway to the world. It must convey a lot about your professional style and capabilities.

Create a statement that explains every single detail about yourself and what you are able to provide. Create a compelling logo that combines the essence of what you do by utilizing an impressive structure. The savvy connection will put you at the top of your game by helping people remember who you are and what you're.

Think about other ways you can Show Your Talent In The World

A professional business card is just one of many devices that are limited in time you can utilize to boost your presentation. It is a good sign. A notice is a great way to show the very most effective of your work.

Be careful not to put the entire contents of your message as it will create an obstacle and will stop viewers from getting an impression of your capabilities. Take note of the place that you could display your message. The proper arrangement of the location of your signage can enhance its impact. It can increase the excitement of your job and allow for more possible possibilities for outcomes.

Make sure to tell people how to connect!

A professional's business card is not just to showcase your creativity; it also serves as an requirement. It should inform potential customers how to contact you. Include all the unique ways to contact you: contact numbers, websites, email numbers, as well as any other internet-based networking website you're associated with. Keep in mind the importance of the internet and bookmarking sites They can allow feature to significantly increase the amount in your job.

You must be flexible

Think about tackling zones that you'd never imagined You'll find something you can do with your talents. This will allow you to build a reputation. Another method of advancing your skills, in addition to using the business card of professionals and other professionals, is to join networks where you provide services for free. Create something that people are likely to see everyday which is an amazing advertising opportunity for your talents. Your work will be able to make it in the eyes of millions of people and it will bring more customers to your business.

How to Do Business with Your Cricut Machine

There are numerous products you can design using Cricut. There are also a myriad of products you can design that are commercially viable. Entrepreneurship for the self-employed is now easier than ever because of the web and the various platforms that make selling your goods an easy task.

It is likely that you have had a glimpse websites that let you to create a store that you own. Etsy is most likely to be the most well-known among these platforms. Starting a store on Etsy is so easy, it's nearly impossible to not be intrigued about setting up a shop for yourself!

With the Cricut cutting machine, creating a variety of items in all kinds and themes to suit any and any occasion, is the aim for the day. Making these projects could be a lot of enjoyment for any avid craftsperson, but if are spending amount of money to purchase the materials to make your project it may be logical to generate an income from them according to the amount you're making and spending.

If you're a fan of crafting and you would prefer to create things with your Cricut rather as opposed to go out, or engage in other pursuits during your free time, it could be the perfect time to. If your craft room is overflowing with projects that you've created, but haven't used them for the occasion you've been planning to attend You might discover that you can sell these items to other people, making more money than you did for the supplies, as well as be compensated for the time you spent to create the project at all!

The benefit of selling your products is that because there isn't a brick and mortar to oversee, and no hours of operation to manage it is possible to manage your sales and projects within the free time you have. It is recommended to begin your business when you have a steady stream of revenue. In this way, as your business expands and expands, you can reduce the size when it becomes necessary to work according to your typical work schedule to give you more time to work on your store.

How do you find your Focus?

Determine where your most intense passion and talents intersect with ways to help your viewers. Find a solution the issue. Be specific about the solution you can offer. Don't try to think in general terms; make sure to think about the specifics of what you are planning to write about.

Set up certain categories, topics, and posts you'll create, to draw in a specific group of people and provide them with information in a way that is relevant. Plan them out so that you can start planning your pins right away. It is also possible to brainstorm the products or services you could offer in addition. Make sure you are specific in your thoughts.

Set up Your Business

The Name you choose

Selecting a name is the first step to set up your business since it will be required for the following steps. It may seem easy, but often this is the most difficult part of beginning! The name you choose for your business seems like a personal choice and should reflect you and your work and also to stand out. When choosing a business's name there are many aspects to take into consideration:

* Does it seem easy to comprehend?

* Is it simple to pronounce?

* Is it used?

occasion you've been planning to attend You might discover that you can sell these items to other people, making more money than you did for the supplies, as well as be compensated for the time you spent to create the project at all!

The benefit of selling your products is that because there isn't a brick and mortar to oversee, and no hours of operation to manage it is possible to manage your sales and projects within the free time you have. It is recommended to begin your business when you have a steady stream of revenue. In this way, as your business expands and expands, you can reduce the size when it becomes necessary to work according to your typical work schedule to give you more time to work on your store.

How do you find your Focus?

Determine where your most intense passion and talents intersect with ways to help your viewers. Find a solution the issue. Be specific about the solution you can offer. Don't try to think in general terms; make sure to think about the specifics of what you are planning to write about.

Set up certain categories, topics, and posts you'll create, to draw in a specific group of people and provide them with information in a way that is relevant. Plan them out so that you can start planning your pins right away. It is also possible to brainstorm the products or services you could offer in addition. Make sure you are specific in your thoughts.

Set up Your Business

The Name you choose

Selecting a name is the first step to set up your business since it will be required for the following steps. It may seem easy, but often this is the most difficult part of beginning! The name you choose for your business seems like a personal choice and should reflect you and your work and also to stand out. When choosing a business's name there are many aspects to take into consideration:

* Does it seem easy to comprehend?

* Is it simple to pronounce?

* Is it used?

* Does it define the business's mission?

* Is it unique?

After you've decided on the name that matches the criteria above You must be sure that it's not currently in use. A simple way to confirm this is to use an internet as well as a social media or search. Type the name of your business into the search box on the internet and then read the results that appear. If the name isn't yet in use Repeat the process on the most popular social media platforms like Instagram, Pinterest, and Facebook. Etsy is another website to look up. Sometimes, the pages of these platforms will be displayed in a search engine however it's an excellent idea to verify.

Legal Actions

If there is no one else using the exact name you've picked It's time to sign up as a company! There are a variety of business models to pick from, and the one that is right for you is dependent on your specific needs. It is recommended to talk to an attorney for this decision however small-scale firms are generally sole proprietorships, or limited liability companies (LLCs). If you are a sole proprietor is a personal responsibility, you will be accountable for the business's finances and assets, however you still have the option to apply for a trade mark. Sole proprietorships work well for businesses with low risk. Through an LLC the personal assets of your business would be separated from your company's assets, and would not be at risk in the event that your business gets declared bankrupt or sued. In either case, you'll be required to file paperwork in your county, and perhaps get permits to operate within your state. An attorney or The Small Business Administration (SBA) and the county clerk's office are excellent resources for registering your company.

Before proceeding the name of your business must be registered at the office of the county clerk. Each county has its own rules however it typically involves an easy form and an amount of under $50. Registration with the county is essential to be in a position to establish bank accounts for business, obtain permits as well as collecting tax on sales. If you are operating a company, it's important to ensure that you collect tax on sales. To legally collect taxes the company will have registration with the government. This is an easy procedure, and forms are usually filled out on the website of the state comptroller. Once you've been declared your business it will grant you a permit. The business must prepare quarterly sales tax returns and pay taxes. The information on how to do this is available on the website of the state comptroller.

Policies

Small craft businesses tend to overlook the importance of having policies in place. Policies provide a detailed explanation of the way your company handles issues that might arise when it comes to fulfilling orders for customers. The existence of specific policies can help you identify issues with customer service. Similar to how large retailers publish the policies on their websites, in customer services areas, or on receipts Yours should be easily accessible as well. Policies can be displayed on your website or social media platforms, and handed out to customers when they place an order. When writing your policies, be certain to include items like shipping, deposits return, processing times. It is possible that additional policies will need to be included as time passes and new issues come up. Many small-scale craft companies begin by accepting orders from small-scale local region, but you could discover yourself fulfilling orders from distant customers as time passes. It's also possible to begin selling online, and in this scenario the majority of customers could be outside of your local area. In any case, including concerns concerning shipping into your policies is crucial. Consider questions such as:

* Can you ship orders outside of the United States? This may incur additional costs as well as VAT taxes and can cause a lot of confusion.

What are the shipping expenses? You can find out at usps.gov. If you only make a few kinds of products (for instance, all you create is a custom ornament) It is straightforward to figure out a set price for all. If, however, your company makes a variety of products with a range of sizes, you might need to declare that the cost of shipping will be based on the item. If that's the case, you should be sure to inform your customers about the price when they make an order.

How do you ship items (priority first class, priority etc.)? Do you offer tracking?

What happens in the event that an item is lost? Who is responsible for its replacement? If the item you purchased is not delivered, can you offer the item in exchange for settling to the company that shipped the item? The tracking of shipments is recommended so that you can verify the delivery.

Inventory

The ability to keep track of inventory throughout the year can help with tax preparation later. There are a variety of software to help you manage your inventory, however I've discovered that spreadsheets work well for my little crafting business. It is important to keep track of every item you have in your inventory and the amount the cost per item is for each category of items. Consult a tax professional for more information.

Logo

One last thing to consider when setting your small craft company is to create an identity. It will be your brand's identity and how customers will perceive your product, therefore it is essential to include the logo printed on everything from business cards, social media packaging, bags of products and stickers, among others. The logo should be representative of your company's image and the way you would like to be associated with it. It must be contemporary and contemporary. Make sure that the colors are consistent and incorporate them across all areas of your company. If you're stuck making a logo, search for ideas from different sources. There are stores on Etsy as well as other websites that offer ready-made logos for companies. Graphic designers in your area can help , but typically, it comes at a price of around hundred dollars. It could be worth it as graphic designers will take your suggestions and integrate the ideas into a distinctive logo.

Pricing Products

The most frequent query I receive is "What should I charge for my services? ...?" Most often, this question is asked following the fact that the person has already created custom items for a client. There are many methods to determine what you should charge, but the most important thing is to ensure that you are able to recover the costs for your time and experience. Make a decision on the cost before creating the item and ensure the client is aware of the cost. Pricing can be a challenge if you're making the project for a family or friend member, but it's crucial to keep in mind that you can't offer goods or services for free, but yet make a decent income. It is possible to offer discounts to relatives or friends, but be sure you can sustain it.

Taxes on Income

Tax professionals can help you figure out what to declare as profits and expenses for your taxes on income, however there are things you need to keep on top of throughout the year, in order to aid in preparing your tax returns. From these, expenses like expenses, mileage and inventory come quickly to your mind. The way I track my expenses is as described in the previous paragraph However, I also classify my expenses to facilitate tax preparation. You might need to categorize your expenses in categories like items, postage, taxes, or other items that you pay for.

Business Banking

It is crucial for you to maintain your corporate accounts distinct from your personal accounts. Certain banks will provide free business checking to customers who have a minimum balance and have the least amount of features. I have found these useful for my company. The bank might also offer additional services, like the debit card or online banking. You can also make effortless transfers between your company as well as personal account.

With the money you have in your bank account for business you can also decide to put it in your company. This could mean upgrading equipment, buying products in bulk in order to save money in the future and anything else which could benefit your company in the long term. For a business in the field of vinyl crafting you might need to purchase a bigger heating press or a number of cutting machines to improve the efficiency of your work.

The Ethics of Business, Copyright and Trademark

Copyright is usually applied to things like books or pieces of art. Trademarks are typically used to describe words and logos - objects that are used to identify the brand. Sometimes, you may be asked to create it for a client. When creating items or working with a client it is essential to be mindful of respecting the work of other creators and not use their designs to create your own. They can be cartoon characters or company logos. It is not legal to incorporate the elements you have chosen to use within your designs without the permission of the designer. It can be tempting to promote a beautiful design by using the logo of a local sport team, as it will probably be a hit however, you shouldn't make this mistake or anything similar to it. If you're unsure whether a request from a client is copyrighted or trademarked you can check the online database of the government. Many crafters break the rules of trademarks and copyright even though it may not be apparent that it is important however, it does for the ethics of your business. Be sure to seek legal advice if you are still unclear about creating an item that is potentially trademarked/copyrighted.

The most important thing to remember about ethics in the field of craft is to be authentic and truthful about your skills. Make sure that you are able to provide what you have promised to the customer, without using someone else's trademarked/copyrighted ideas. The most effective method to stand out in this industry is to be original and innovative!

Chapter 6: How To Earn Money With Your Cricut

In terms of earning money at your home, it is easy to can do this using a Cricut. But, you must be aware that there are lots of rivals so you need to make extra efforts to have the chance of succeeding.

Change the Hobby into a small business

Making your passion into a profitable small-business might sound like a thrilling possibility, but if you don't plan properly it, you'll end up failing.

Be aware of your options before you leap and take on the responsibility of money, time effort, and motivation is the best method to ensure that your company.

Beginning a new venture could be intimidating however, with proper preparation and the right foundation, you'll be more certain of the success.

If you're successful then your entire family will succeed. Others in the same community may be successful.

If you're concerned about the current economic situation and, let's admit it that is the case today, then starting an enterprise as a part-time job or an investing in the future could provide the support you need to weather the storm.

If you can plan a bit and foresight and you'll be able to transform your hobby into a profitable business and then grow from a hobby that you enjoy part-time to a full-time, profitable small-scale enterprise.

You can do working from home, particularly orders that are placed on the internet, and then turn the work into a profitable profession that you can work from any point around the globe.

It is possible to use websites like Etsy to begin selling your items. Perhaps one day you'll have your own personal website that is perfect for your company and its products.

Utilizing the latest technologies available through the internet You can earn money all day, every day of every year, even if you're sick or on vacation.

Best of luck for your new venture as a fresh small-business owner.

It is beneficial when you earn a an income part-time from something you enjoy doing. You can have enjoyable designing while earning money from it. You could turn this into an excellent business that will earn you a lot of money in one month and cover the expenses of your family. If you own a Cricut in your home and and you aren't making the most of it and you're able to spare enough time, then this article will provide a great benefit to you.

How to turn your designs to cash

A lot of people have these questions:

* "How can I earn money with the Cricut?"

* "Should I invest in an Cricut or are the markets overcrowded?"

* "Can I still earn money? How do I start?"

It can be difficult to find a satisfactory answer to these concerns, as certain people who use Cricut don't want to give you tips on how you can earn money with this craft. They don't want to divulge their secrets. However, this book is here to provide you with all the details that you must know for making profits with Cricut.

A lot of people get started, and they begin to explore a craft perhaps they own an Cricut or other cutting machine for vinyl; or they might not have one , but want to buy one. They are flooded with questions regarding how to start and can be overwhelming initially. It's often complex and confusing. And it is not uncommon to contact people who already have one. They don't want to divulge their secrets as they fear they will be able to compete with you. The truth is that everybody can succeed when you build one another up. There is room for all of us to be successful. Let's begin by asking the first question.

Let's now look at how we can earn money from the information we've acquired. If you are unable to make money with the information you've gathered or if you already have the information but it is useless or useful to your needs, that knowledge is of no use to you or society. To ensure that this knowledge to be useful to you, I'll teach you how to earn profits from it. However, this doesn't mean that when you're not making profits from your designs that the information isn't worth it particularly if you are using it for only your family and your friends. If you only use it to help your friends and family it is beneficial.

Is the market saturated?

A lot of us are many of us are on Facebook We go to marketplaces, and you might have been to Etsy and seen a lot of shops selling posters, selling shirts, selling something or another, you're thinking, how is it possible to make money through my work? The short answer to the question is that yes you can and it's not too difficult. Find what you're good at and keep it up. There are a lot of things you could do that you can do, and we've identified 50 of them in this book you can begin with. Choose one of the 50 listed or search online start with one and continue to work on it until you are a pro in the field. With every person specialized in the particular area that he is able to improve and the market will never be overcrowded. For instance, a person might specialize in only the production of T-shirts. Another might specialize is in the making of cups, a third in woodwork designs or woodwork design, etc. In reality, you won't find anyone who is skilled in a specific area. This means that the market could never be full.

What is the best place to start?

When you've purchased your Cricut, you are wondering where to begin. The best place to begin is by creating things for family and friends. There are a myriad of things you can make for your friends that they will be delighted and even pay for. Some examples are creating stickers, designing their name on T-shirts writing inspirational words on their T-shirts and so on. It is possible to think of some ideas they will appreciate and begin designing the design for them. You could also design designs for your children and spouse. After you've finished with the designs, share them on Facebook You may get those who would like you to create the same thing for them. This is the most efficient method to start with a design if nobody is buying the design from you, but without investing a lot of money.

Making Crafts to Sell By Using Cricut

There are plenty of things that we have mentioned in the past that you could start doingand then selling to your neighbors and friends. It is not necessary be able to persuade your buddies to purchase all of these items since I'm sure they'll be happy when you create your own plans for them. What you need to do is figure the things your buddies are interested in and create an image for them. For instance, if you have a friend who enjoys football and is part of teams, you can create your team's logo to use as stickers for this person, and then write something positive about the team to him or her as well. If you have a close friend who sews clothes and you like the work he does then you can create an attractive design using his or her company's name. You can also make an emblem of their logo to wear on every clothing item he/she designs.

Another way to make money from your designs is to search for people who want you to iron your designs on their clothing for them. There are plenty of people searching for someone who can create designs on their clothes for them. Find the designers who sell their products in boutiques and offer your designs to them. This is how it's done. You could offer an original design for someone who sells lots of plain T-shirts and inform them of that you've created something they'll appreciate. If they love the design You can offer them a price that you'd like in exchange for each design you create for them. Therefore, you should look for local vendors that you think would be interested in your style.

Another way that you earn money selling to groups. It is possible to walk up to an audience of people who wears a uniform and an official name for the group, and request their group's logo. This is simple as each member of the group wants to be recognized as belonging to the group and will want to pay the designer for their work. Some examples of these groups are choirs, clubs and associations of friends etc. The most effective way to do this is to an unpaid design to the head of your group in the beginning. The concept behind this is that when you are able to get the attention of the person in charge by your concept, you will be able to quickly sell your design to all members of the group. In addition, the members of the group will see the design of the leader's desk, and they will be asking him where he created the design. A few will even suggest why not create the design for all of them. After that, he'll be required to design the layout for each person on the team. Make the leader enthusiastic and you'll be able to get the attention of the group quickly.

Another excellent way to sell your work online is to sell it on. You can make your own website and sell what you design on the site or sell it through online stores such as Amazon. Most people are online nowadays, therefore you won't find it difficult to sell your designs if they're beautiful and appealing.

How to become a Cricut Affiliate

You can be an Cricut affiliate by creating an instructional video for their website. If you've got a large following on social media, you could be an affiliate. If you have an online following and are interested in becoming an Cricut affiliate (click here now to sign up). If you go to that website you must register for an affiliate programme. After signing up and have completed the registration process, you'll be able to generate an affiliate link you can give to others who use the link. Those who click on it receives a payment for you. Therefore, if you have an online blog, YouTube channel or the physical presence of students you coach and a large group of telegrams or WhatsApp You can use your affiliate link to share with these groups.

How to Save Money When Utilizing Your Cricut Explore Machine for business

For those who are new to the craft it is this part which causes the most trouble, particularly when your wallet isn't adequate to store your materials for crafting and projects. Therefore, I'd like to offer suggestions on how you can make the most of the Cricut Explore machine for your business and purchase your supplies at the most affordable prices. Don't be ripped off of the money you've earned longer.

First, learn the instruction manual regarding how to use the Cricut Explore machine correctly. It's not just to be used as a source of entertainment that manufacturers put instruction manuals on their products. It's designed to aid you in getting maximum benefit from your equipment. Follow the directions carefully and you'll get a little more cash which could have been put towards repairs or a the purchase of a new one.

It is recommended to have to replace your cutting mat dependent on use at times. It is recommended to use the 12-inch by 24 inches mat because long mats will help you save cost. It is possible to flip it over on its other side as the adhesive strength on the original side begins to decrease. Instead of purchasing a new one you can flip it and then continue your next project.

Blades' price will drain your budget if you don't make most of them. I'm not required to explain the importance of having a sharp blade for cutting. If you want to save money, you must take good maintenance of your knives. keep them in order and don't use the blade to cut improper materials. Anything that is contrary to this could mean you'll have to replace your blade frequently and that means money is draining out of your pocket.

For your vinyl items I would suggest using Expressions Vinyl, which is less expensive than other vinyl options and offers the same look to your work.

It is beneficial to earn a some money from what you love doing. You could be having enjoyment with your design but still make profits from the design. There are plenty of people earning money from their designs. It is possible to turn this into an excellent business that will bring in a lot of money in one month and cover all the family costs. So, if you own a Cricut at home, but you're not getting the most out of the useof it, and have the time, this section can provide a great benefit to you.

To be success in the Cricut world of crafting You must keep these tips in your mind.

Dare to Be Different

You must be who you are to express your quirky side and imagination.

People who have been around the world of Cricut-craft for a long time will be familiar with the name tiles that knock out. They were a huge hit and soon everyone was making and selling the tiles.

In the craft world this is the standard. So, you might be among the first to join trends and follow the trend until the next hot item comes along. But be aware that the strategy of selling Cricut items can turn expensive and exhausting if you aren't careful.

Keep It Short

A lot of craftspeople think that making and selling anything every conceivable thing leads to an increase in patronage, and therefore more cash, but this is not the way it works. In fact it can create a massive inventory of products that are not sold, which leads to more burning out and a high cost. Instead of producing products in a few places instead, you must concentrate on becoming the best in your field of craftsmanship to ensure that when people require certain products within your region you are the one they turn to you.

Follow The Holiday

There are certain items you can create specifically for a day to make it easier for you to sell. For instance, for Valentine's Day, you might create the adorable funny underwear, or even the monkeys.

It is also possible to make vases. You can also purchase a Christmas cap and add an attractive style on it.

Make Your Work Public

It is not enough to post just a couple of photos and hope that it will be an portfolio. Make sure you have the best outline and work in advance, achieve a high level of artistic proficiency and then upload your work into Instagram, Facebook, or an artist's website. People like seeing galleries of work.

In the end people will be enthralled to see your work and will not be able to wait long for you to share your latest drawing or work.

Broaden Your Horizons

Maybe web design isn't for you, but this is just one of the models. It is also possible to create your art work into prints and shirts, scratch pad and more. You can take the visual communication program and create artwork for groups or groups. One of the best ways to broaden your perspective is to turn your knowledge into teaching. Teaching gives you credibility in your field, but increases your earnings because of the fact that, aside from earning money from your classes or books, you also get to show your presentation a polished look and can help you negotiate deals as well.

Be Consistent

Don't publish a photo of your work disappearing for two months and then expecting customers to start pounding on your door is not the right approach. If you are required to negotiate deals, you need to be trustworthy. There's only a limited amount of time that you can spend to be on a newsfeed before your message gets lost in the noise and replaced by newer and more relevant content. Therefore regardless of whether or not it is dull in your head try posting something that is similar in a few days.

Don't stress about the fact that you are pushing or exaggerating. Just do a well-intentioned update every now and again. This will put what you have to convey on the back of people's minds.

If you are looking to become successful, you need to constantly work to improve improving your Cricut crafts business. Some individuals work only every week, or at least once to sell their products for fun; however If you are planning to build your company, you must to be on the job all day long.

If you are working on other projects and are unable to work all day it is recommended that you create an agenda for the week and adhere to it. If you don't work on your business for months or even weeks at a stretch, you'll never be able to move on in it.

Be Tenacious

It's not an easy task to run a successful business because it takes many hours of hard work, sweat and heartbreaks. So, it is essential keep in mind it is likely to happen times that you'll be tempted to throwing your towel in the air. There will be days where things don't go as planned.

However, it is essential to consider the bigger overall picture because crafting isn't an opportunity to make money fast. Keep in mind that those who quit do not win, therefore quitting is not an alternative. Do what you enjoy, and continue getting better. Successful people never give up. They have many failures, but they never give up.

Learn Everyday

Learn from those who have had success in their business. It's not essential to figure everything out on your own as whatever you're working on, others have done it in the past.

If you're looking to figure out how to create a profitable Facebook community, or learn how to rise up in the Etsy selling ranks you should remember that others have done this in the past and are sharing their strategies and tricks they have learned.

Quality Control

If you are planning to increase the size of your brand, it is essential to focus on the sale of top-quality products. The motto you should follow is 'quality over all else.'

You don't want to be recognized as one who produces low-quality items, since if the word gets out (and it will surely) your company's image is likely to be closed.

If you concentrate your attention and effort on the creation of top-quality materials, you'll be able to stand up to competition regardless of how tough it may be.

6. Working with Customers

Craft businesses like yours wouldn't have the success they enjoy today in the absence of our loyal customers particularly frequent customers. As such, our customer support is the foundation of my business. There are numerous options customers can select for payment. A lot of customers prefer electronic methods for making payments. This is particularly beneficial if they are looking to reduce the need for several trips (making the deposit , then collecting their merchandise). PayPal as well as Square are both good choices to receive payments. A majority of my electronic payments are made via PayPal as it permits me to issue an invoice. Customers can pay on the internet using their personal PayPal and credit cards. Although a fee may be to be charged, you must permit the client to pay as a business transaction, as it's an official transaction. The price you charge should be sufficient to cover charges that come with the costs of conducting business. It is not legal to charge an additional fee. With a proof of the payment made for services and goods and the owner of the business as well as the client are secure. Square is simple to use and also.

Undecided Customers

We've all encountered an order from a client who did not have an idea of what they want on a t-shirt, for instance. After a few texts and emails we're left to wonder whether the venture is worthwhile at this moment. There are alternatives to help aid customers in making choices.

It's beneficial to have a plan of action for clients who can't decide to purchase a product, in order to inform them of the number of changes you're willing to make to an idea, prior to a cost for design is imposed. Of course, design costs are applied to an end product but it's helpful to ensure that customers are committed to all changes they're willing make. I prefer to permit two distinct changes at the same time with the same design fee. Customers are able to alter several features of the layout in each modification. For instance, during one instance, the client might choose a different font, request a different design or color, and then choose another.

If you're not selling on a platform like Etsy which accepts payments in advance and we'll all experience this problem eventually. The most efficient way to collect your money quicker is to use online payment providers like PayPal that allow your customers to pay in a matter of minutes. Also, putting an upfront deposit like we mentioned earlier is a way to identify the clients who aren't serious about buying the item. However easy we make it, it's possible for a buyer to not remember their checkbook or to send the cash later and not pay. This can help you keep an eye on who has and hasn't paid, and you can issue a reminder at the close of the month to those who truly forgot to pay. It is also possible to send customers an invoice using PayPal and allow customers to pay online using a credit card.

Nobody likes to ask the money of their customers, yet it's certain that we'll have to ask for it at some time. By requesting a deposit in advance and offering a simple method to pay the amount will help safeguard you and inspire your clients to purchase their goods.

Pricing Problems

The majority of people realize that hand-crafted, exclusive products aren't affordable. The owners of craft businesses must be aware of our materials and the hourly wage, but that's not discounted prices. The final decision is dependent on the individual customer. certain customers do not have the funds to invest. However, my suggestion when speaking to clients who wish to negotiate prices is to never lower the price in the event that you are able to. Make sure you take the cost of the materials as well as your hourly wage into account. Make sure to emphasize what makes your handcrafted product unique. In the long term it's not worth the risk to sacrifice yourself in order to gain a sale since you'll lose money and customers will begin to expect lower costs.

The Pickup Process is a bit difficult

Many craft-related businesses do not have a retail storefront however, only a handful of us participate in festivals or markets where customers purchase items in person. This is why it is sometimes difficult to schedule an appointment or pick-up place for both your customers and you. There may be customers who do not want to set aside the trip to pick up the order they placed with you. It is likely that you have the deposit to ensure that you do not be able to lose money on supplies, and you'll only lose the time you spend (Have I already mentioned that deposits are crucial?). When an order is cancelled then you may offer the item for sale or donate it or even give it away (gift raffles, raffles or social media contests and door prize at these events) and let the client know that they're approaching the expiration date.

Unsatisfied With The Product

The policy for refunds should be clear in advance. I suggest that you offer refunds only if the item isn't customized (so it can be sold again) as well as if the fault is yours. Personalized items are not resold or resold. If the item is produced as you requested All sales are final. But, nobody is perfect and sometimes we make mistakes. If you've made a mistake, then the most effective option is to reimburse the customer or even redo the mistake for free. If the customer decides to get a refund or a redo, they should send the product back. The exception is when the buyer provided the blank (a shirt as an instance) and you then put the sticker on. In this instance I believe it's right for the customer to retain the shirt was bought. Sometimes, it is more sensible to make a new order for the client. It is usually a rare instance where you've completed the order in accordance with the request and the customer is not happy with the way it appears when they see it in the person.

One way to avoid having to cancel an order is to save copies of every communication between you and your customer and to provide evidence prior to the production of the product.

Know when to leave

When a client is concerned or has a question I will try to respond according to my guidelines, while being polite and respectful. If there's disagreement that is not common and rare, we will always come up with a solution using communicating. If you anticipate these scenarios and preparing in advance it is possible to talk to your customer without emotional or defensive. Communication is essential to solve problems with customer service and customer satisfaction is crucial. Be aware that we must never react in anger or out of frustration regardless of whether we believe that we have a right to do so. Any communication you send or text or do can be posted online for eternity, and may harm your company's reputation.

Chapter 7: Where To Sell Items You've Made By Your Cricut?

If you are planning to sell your products before you sell your products on Etsy I would suggest that you set up your own website first, and then sell your items on Etsy. Etsy is a platform that allows people to sell their antique handmade, custom or even unique products. There are a lot of people who are selling their crafts and you are able to join them to sell your own. You can then take your Etsy and put it on the pinboard to be seen by customers to see on Pinterest too. Your images must be impressive to draw customers to purchase your item. It is well known that buyers purchase looks before buying your actual products.

Vendor Markets

One of the quickest methods of earning a amount of money is to take part in an outdoor market for vendors particularly during the fall months or prior to the holiday season. At this time of the season, people are keeping their eyes on gifts and there are lots of events and markets to take part in. It is a great opportunity to meet new customers, increase exposure and meet other vendors.

There are a lot of aspects to take into consideration when deciding whether or not you'd like to take part in an open market. Although it is possible to earn quick cash because your customers are all together and expect to buy something, you should be prepared ahead of time. Before you commit to taking part it is important to consider:

* Set-up Do you have enough space to showcase your items in a pleasant manner? Does the space contain everything you require for your booth (electricity and Wi-Fi, for instance.)? What does your booth's look like?

* Time commitment: Are you capable of preparing prior to the date? Will you be at markets for whole period?

* Security for your money - Don't leave your money in the open!

* Cost of upfront - Many market require booth rental cost. It is also necessary to prepare your products prior to the event.

* Payment - How do you accept payments? Are you equipped with the capability to accept payment via electronic methods like Square, PayPal, etc. ?

* Assistants: Is there someone who could help you to set up, manage the booth, or pack up?

There are many markets that are not created to be equal. Some attract huge crowds while others draw fewer customers. To determine which are the best for you I suggest talking with other vendors who have taken part. This will help you determine whether a market merits the effort, time and time it takes to take part.

If you choose to set up an exhibit at a fair, make certain to be able to connect with your clients. Keep many business cards in your possession as well as your social media accounts as well as your email address. You might want to consider offering free samples like small decals created from scrap vinyl or even an auction to bring people to your stand. Make sure you interact with customers welcoming them and providing assistance. Nothing can cause a customer to leave faster than a business that shows no interest in their customers.

Social Media

With platforms like Instagram, Facebook, Pinterest through platforms such as Facebook, Instagram, Pinterest, and YouTube through these platforms, you can promote your product, interact with your customers from all over the globe, and gain knowledge from business owners who are also entrepreneurs. It's free, simple and effective. The more comments, likes and followers you've got more people be able to see your posts. These apps also allow paid advertisements to advertise your company and get it in front of more users. After your account for business is created you can upload photos and videos and send messages and receive them, and receive notifications regarding likes and comments. You can also access analytical information which shows the number of people who have seen your posts, as well as other data.

All this information is accessible through your smartphone or computer. You can make the projects you come across easy and then post photos of it online, notifying to your friends that the item is available for purchase. This will ensure that the person who is buyingthe item, will view the photo of the item they are purchasing prior to placing an order for it. Customized crafts should be part of your purchase order. Facebook is the most likely one that the majority of us are familiar withsince it's been around for longer than any of the other. Alongside creating a business page to advertise your products and services, you can also set up an account for a group. In the event that you are managing a group you can decide who's in it, and you are able to create posts that only members can view. It provides privacy if you would like it however it also lets you to make your posts targeted towards your target audience.

Instagram is another application that is popular. The importance of hashtags and followers is in making your content visible to larger audiences. They is possible to link your Facebook account which allows you to publish the Instagram posts directly to Facebook without the need to recreate them in Facebook. Facebook application. The more likes, hashtags, and followers you post the more people are likely to be able to see them.

Pinterest and YouTube are useful tools too, though I've never had an order that was prompted by either. I believe that these platforms will be useful in reaching out to clients who are seeking tutorials and suggestions that could be the direction you'd prefer to take your business. A lot of people earn money from YouTube channels when advertisers agree to promote their channels.

We're all aware of how social media has turned into an effective marketing tool for not just established companies as well as small-scale enterprises and budding entrepreneurs. Just add hashtags to sell or selling products samples, free shipping, samples included, and many more, to attract prospective buyers. Join Facebook's Community pages and groups for sellers and buyers of handcrafted products to promote your items. Utilize catchy phrases such as "customization is available at no additional fee' and 'for free refunds for any customer who is not happy, when posting your items on these pages, as well as your own Facebook page. Make use of Twitter to share the feedback of your happy customers to expand your customers' base. This can be done by creating a satisfaction questionnaire that you can send to buyers, or even include an image of your Etsy listing, and asking for online reviews and feedback from your clients.

Another thing to remember is to upload photos of all you've made using Cricut machines, including those that you didn't intend to sell. There is no way to know who could need something that you felt was not worth selling. Because you'll be making them after an order has been made and you have the ability to collect the necessary supplies following the order and begin making.

Target Local Farmer's Markets And Boutiques

If you enjoy the excitement of a show and tell, make a reservation for a booth at a local market for farmers, and be there with craft items that are ready to sell. In this scenario you're counting on the amount of people that attend, and the subset of people who are looking to purchase from your booth. If you live in a city area in which people are ardently fascinated by distinctive art designs, but don't have the time to make these on their own, you can achieve a huge profit by setting a fair price for your items.

Make flyers available to guests, so that they can contact you via the social networks you have accounts or emails and look through your Etsy listings. Consider the events you host as method of advertising for people who aren't as active on social media, but who can be enthralled by personalized items to help them prepare for their next life occasion like a baby showers, birthday parties or wedding.

The downside of taking part with local activities is that they generate of massive exhibits and inventory which can be costly for loading and shipping the merchandise. It is possible that you won't be in a position to sell all the inventory, based on the scale of the event. However, as I mentioned earlier, you can get the most value by promoting your product and establishing your local customer base.

Online Selling Platforms

The most well-known online seller platform for hand-crafted items is likely Etsy however there are other options, such as Amazon Handmade. Before you start your online store it is recommended to read the manual of the website and decide whether the cost is worthwhile for you. Online stores require a thorough understanding of SEO so that your products are found in the other items and there's lots of competition! They are simple to manage since the site is designed for your use, and the customers are already enticed by the site. The shop cannot be running itself, however it will require an amount of effort and time from the owner of the shop. Descriptions, photos SEO, and photos all require some energy and time.

Consignment and Wholesale

A lot of the owners of vinyl craft businesses can sell their merchandise through consignment or wholesale. Wholesale arrangements mean that you offer your product for sale at a reduced cost to another business owner (usually the owner of a shop) and they will sell the item at a higher price and retain the profits. It's a bit more distinct than consignment. In a consignment scenario, you store your goods in a front of the store, and then price them as you'd like. If your merchandise sells the owner of the store keeps the percentage (usually 20% to 30 percent) while you get the remaining amount generated by the sale.

There's pros as well as cons for consignment and wholesale. The main benefit of such arrangements is the fact that your products are displayed and featured in a retail store, which draws customers in which could lead to higher sales. Customers also are more likely to learn about your company and purchase from you in the future in the event that they want to support local businesses. One of the drawbacks to wholesale and consignment is deciding whether the work is worth the amount you get in the return. It is important to determine the price to offer your merchandise wholesale or on consignment to make a decent profit that is worthy of your time and effort. There is also the possibility that the shop draws only a few customers, meaning your products that are stocked sell. If you are able to sell your products for consignment or wholesale, ensure that you have a signed agreement between you and the owner of the shop to avoid any future issues.

Whatever way you choose to promote your product ensure that you adhere to the law regarding trademarks and copyright and file your tax returns.

Each of these methods are awash with competition, therefore finding your niche and what is it that makes you stand out is the goal to be played. The market research process can aid you in you determine who your customers are searching for, which could aid in developing your products around those who purchase from you. For instance my primary clients are females seeking unique shirts and gifts, so I attempt to keep up-to-date with the current trends in these areas. I then promote my merchandise on social media, which attracts customers. I've noticed that even though my customers can purchase customized shirts and other gifts online They like the convenience and the customer service I provide.

eBay

You could upload your creations on eBay and then sell them on eBay.

Join Cricut Affiliate to become a Cricut Affiliate

It is a way to pay to create tutorial videos for Cricut the maker of these videos. These videos are posted on the internet for online user to access. To be an affiliate Cricut associate, you have to have a solid web presence. Additionally, you must have a specific amount of people following your Facebook and Twitter profiles.

Post Tutorial Videos On Your Vlog

This is not to have to do with affiliate marketing Instead, you set up an online blog with videos, upload videos for tutorials and earn money by the traffic you generate.

Facebook Groups

This is another great platform to sell your work in. There are many people who have sales every day on Facebook and you could join in too. When your design is stunning and you can take great photos of your designs and then post your images on a Facebook page there are lots of people placing orders for it. If they are willing to purchase from outside your area it is important to be ready to deliver it to them. If you want the group to not view your message as spam, you have be a part of groups which specialize in hand-crafted designs or craft. There are a lot of them available which you can research and join now.

Craft Fairs

It is possible to set up at a craft fair and create a variety of items. Visit a craft fairs in your area where you can find a wide range of hand-crafted items to sell. If you visit this kind of place you are also able to sell your work there.

Earning Money Teaching

There are many of your friends that have bought a Cricut and aren't aware of how to operate it. A lot of them may have bought it, but must be taught how to use it effectively. That's where you need to be present to teach users how to use the machine, as well as how to make specific designs. The art of creating designs using Cricut isn't limited to just face-to-face interaction. You can create YouTube channels and instruct many people how to create designs. The advantage of having the YouTube account is that users will let you know what they think they should be teaching them. Many will tell you what the next video you ought to create.

If you are teaching them through YouTube You will not earn money directly from them , except the case that they send you some advice. However, you are able to earn money through affiliate marketing. A lot of them are likely to watch your channel but don't yet have a Cricut and are looking to purchase one. If they purchase through an affiliate hyperlink, you'll get a percentage of the purchase. The benefit of affiliate marketing through Amazon is that even if your customer clicks on the Cricut machine and goes to Amazon website, but purchases something else that is interesting to the person and you are still paid for the purchase of your customer. This is the reason why I suggest that you do not be an affiliate partner with the Cricut company alone; you should also establish your affiliate program with Amazon.

Chapter 8: Project Ideas

In the world of scrapbooking, some may think there are only devices that are hardware, such as the Cricut cutting machine and Cricut Expression machine. There are, however, software tools that can assist you in creating incredible Cricut ideas that can aid in creating your perfect scrapbook.

One that stands out is The Cricut Design Studio. The application offers a new method of connecting your original machine to your computer and, indeed, it's able to utilize every Cricut word machine.

With the help of cutting mats that are on screen, this tool creates cuts and designs, as well as navigating the whole Cricut Cartridge Library. One of the advantages of this is that the images you see are exactly the cut you made! This tool is equipped with an interface that is user-friendly and has the ability to save all of your work. Every scrapbooker should have this software!

This device can make anything and create numerous Cricut ideas. The principle is that you should let your creativity run that there are no boundaries. When you make your own scrapbook, the main purpose is to design designs that will be incorporated into the photos you put in.

Let's say, for instance, you add pictures that you took of the wedding. You have to choose or design an aesthetic that will create an atmosphere that could inspire anyone who views your scrapbooks and photos remember the day. The same fundamental rule applies to all. It is also possible to earn income through helping people think of ideas for their scrapbook.

The software program isn't restricted to only creating scrapbooks. It allows you to use your imagination to define the limits and through the program, there are bound be no boundaries.

The most popular design that originates from the Cricut printer, aside from scrapbooks, are Cricut calendars. It is possible to use the templates that you get from the Cricut machine to add a touch of spice and personality to any calendar.

Utilizing the Cricut computer and its applications tools, you can design layouts for each month of the year. The trick is to select the right design that will concentrate on what the month is all about. Let's take October as an illustration, and the most appealing design will be one that depicts the festival of October. So, there you have some amazing Cricut strategies that can make you money or make you happy. Cricut tasks are ones that you can complete using the Cricut cutter. It is possible to make it from the mundane that can bring you satisfaction and help you earn money. In the past, many considered this printer to be an instrument for scrapbookers. With the ever-growing creativity of mankind, ideas are expanding like crazy.

The users had to understand that the Cricut cutter is just a die-cutting machine. It is not an individual who is responsible for the creation of designs. There are designs available through cartridges and software. Most Cricut printers cut the designs which the user selects from the software or cartridges only. The program that is responsible for creating models for the numerous Cricut-related tasks, is that of the Cricut Design Studio. It has hundreds of designs to select from. You can also create your own designs and alter designs they have available in their library. After you've chosen your preferred design, you can make use of your Cricut machine to cut it out , and you're all set to go.

Cards for greeting cards are just one thing you can use the Cricut machine to cut for. A lot of people come up with their own designs they've thought up and engraved on their minds.

A majority times the mall you go to will not have the design you're seeking. Sometimes, they might be able to, but it's an act of faith. With the complete Cricut machine, you are able to make your own design and be happy with the result.

You can give out cards you design which will earn you money. This is the ideal business-minded mindset for you! This approach can alleviate tension and stress and allow you to achieve an inner peace. Calendars can be an option.

Calendars are comprised of twelve months over the year, and each month is unique to it's own. With the help of the Cricut cutter, you will be able to bring life to the months. Make sure you create or select designs that can inspire the spirit of the month or something else that is connected to them.

Invitations are also great Cricut tasks. You choose a design that matches the event and then you get it cut using by the Cricut cutting device. The most important thing is to not allow your imagination to slack. Keep it up and you'll have more work to do.

Selling Customized Pre-Cut Vinyl

Vinyl is an easy material to work with. It is available in a range of patterns and colors that enhance its reputation. It is possible to create custom labels for glass canisters and containers for anyone who wants to sort out their pantry. Check out the latest trends on the web and alter the labels to suit your needs. Once you've got your labels created the simplest option is to start an Etsy shop. This is completely free and simple to use. It's similar to the process of opening up the doors to an Amazon prime account. If your product is popular there will be buyers who will purchase even without advertisements. If you want to keep the pace high, consider advertising the Etsy listings on Pinterest as well as different social networks. This is a sure method of bringing more customers towards the Etsy shop, as well as turning potential customers into regular customers. A crucial aspect to consider is the photos you'll use in your page.

You are not allowed to utilize any of the images in Design Space. Design Space application, but you must upload your own images that correspond to the item you're selling.

Create a set of five or six names, such as sugar salt, rice beans, oats etc. which could be offered as a standard-sized package. Create a custom-designed package that permits customers to choose any of the words they wish to see to be included on their package. Because these labels weigh nearly zero, shipping can be handled using regular mail, and usually only one postage stamp, based on the address of delivery. Be sure not to use the next-day or two-day delivery option for these labels. Set aside enough time for delivery so that you can design and send the labels with no anxiety. Once you've established your business model, you are able to modify the price and the delivery of the product (more on this later). Take a look at the other Etsy listings to confirm that the price of your product is competitive, and you're drawing enough prospective buyers.

When you've got some traction on the market and you have a good reputation, you can provide additional projects that are based on vinyl, such as design-specific bumpers or heat transfer vinyl designs that customers can apply to their clothing with the standard heating iron. When you've established a following you can alter and personalize your offerings to make a one-stop store for all things vinyl (great name for your upcoming Etsy shop, isn't it?).

Selling Pieces of Finished Work

You could be using your Cricut machines for a wide range of personal projects, including decorating your home, Christmas decorations, personalized clothing and many more. The next time you set out on another of your adventures that result in unique designs, you can create two copies of the project and then create a second item for sale on the Etsy shop. Another benefit is that you'll be in a position to save every project you create in Design Space. Design Space application for future use. If one of your ideas goes viral, you are able to purchase the necessary supplies and then turn your ideas into profitable products. In this method will not only make your original plan to use for personal purposes yield results as well, but you could also earn more than you did to begin with.

Spend your time researching what types of decorations and designs are in fashion in the market and take them as a source of ideas to your next design. The most popular trends in the market are customized cupcake and cake toppers, as well as watercolor designs that could be displayed as stunning wall decor. Cake toppers can be made using cardstock. It is a different material that is easy for beginners, lightweight and easily transported, wrapped in an envelope.

Create and sell Customized Clothing and Accessories

T-shirts that have trendy designs and words are in style these days. You can follow the same approach for selling the vinyl, but increase the ante. You can make sample clothes that has iron-on designs. You can advertise it with slogans such as 'can be further customized for no cost or even transfer the design onto your own clothes and gain traction on the marketplace. Sling bags can be purchased and personalize them with distinctive designs and sell them as finished goods for a price higher as opposed to a boring, plain sling bag.

Think about creating a line items with a common theme such as that of the DC Marvel characters or the Harry Potter movies, and make custom T-shirts, hats as well as baby bodysuits. It is possible to design customized gift bags and party boxes upon request from the buyer. If your product has an established client base, you can receive ideas for your project directly from them, and offer them a cost for your project. What's not to love?

Another major benefit of heat-transfer vinyl, as we mentioned previously is that anyone can apply the design to the clothing they desire with a regular iron. However, you must include instructions for the transfer with the purchase, and let them know exactly how to prepare for the process of heat transfer so as to not harm their clothing. Also, heat-transfer-resistant vinyl can be shipped with an ordinary envelope for mailing.

Design and Sell Stickers

If you're gifted in design and style, crafting individual stickers might be a good opportunity to make a side hustle using your Cricut. They are simple to create and there are plenty of themes and concepts you could think of to design distinctive designs.

Design and Sell Cell Phone Cases

From superheroes to quotes from superheroes to colors, the sky is the limit when creating unique, one-of-a kind cases for your cell phone. Start with customizing cases for your loved ones and friends.

Design and Sell Nail Decals

If you are a fan of taking care of your nails, you're aware of an market for unique and cute designs for your fingernails. This is a possibility that which not many people have thought of which means you could be among the first to take advantage of this opportunity.

Design and sell Cricut Earrings

If you're comfortable having to weed out tiny cuts from complex designs, you may think about making Cricut earrings.

Window Decals for Design and Sales

Every person has their own unique image of something we're almost obsessed with. A window decal made of vinyl of your favorite image can help in giving your décor an upswing. Selling and making a window decals is a breeze and very profitable.

Make and sell Canvas Wall Art

Wall art that is custom-designed can earn fast and simple cash. Find inspiring quotes or designs and transform these into art to sale.

Create and Sell Onesies

Onesies , also known as bodysuits, are adorable clothing that can be enhanced by using amazing art. Onesies for infants can be designed with lots of text, like "Daddy loves you" or "Momma's baby. Another mushy word art is also a possibility when making onesie designs for children.

Design and sell Hoodies

Hoodies are great for the winter months. The one that is designed will fit more comfortably with youth. It is possible to preorder the design as well.

Design and Sell Design And Sell Leather Neck Piece

A pendant made of leather can be created for as a necklace, and then sold to buyers who are interested. A leather neck piece made of all-leather is also possible to create and offered for sale.

Design and sell banners

Banners can be designed to celebrate holidays, celebrations or camping events and religious events, as well as sporting events. They can all be created and offered for sale.

Design and Sell Window Clings

Window clings that feature the theme of the seasons could be manufactured and then sold. Images or designs could also be used in making window clings.

Design and sell Stencils

Stencils can be designed and sold to those who wish to paint their own sign or a post. This could also bring in some money.

Design and sell Safari Animal Stickers

Safari animal stickers are attractive products. They can be offered to people who love animals. The stickers are simple to create and can be an additional source of revenue production.

Design and Sell Wall Art

The possibilities are endless there. Even with Fixer leading the show, which is which is no longer on and farmhouse wall decor still solid. The site has more than million people searching on Pinterest each month for wall art that is farmhouse. Be sure to not forget about the changes.

Design and Sell Custom-designed Decals

Customized stickers are unique because they can be used for many cease-making utilization of from occasions to decor for your home. If you provide a custom-designed service, it's a distinctiator that bigger stores can't match.

Design and Sell Kids-Related-Wall Decals

Children love decorating throughout the year. From birthday parties to nurseries and toddler birthday showers there's an unending need to decorate your child's room.

Design and Sell Wedding Decorations and Favors

It is a thriving industry for weddings and it's no wonder. As per Pinterest weddings in the backyard are trending upwards. The style of weddings has increased by 441 percent. Everybody wants to store some of their wedding.

Print and Design Paper Flowers

Like farmhouse decor, the popularity of paper planters is on the rise and there are more than 500 million search results related to the subject on Pinterest every month. They're perfect for any occasions, from Mother's Day to weddings to baby showers. This is not surprising because they are so in popular.

Create and sell Cricut Cake Toppers

Cupcake and cake toppers could be the most cost-effective and simple item to make. Parents are constantly trying to improve their game for kids' birthday parties, with a variety of customized decorations.

Unicorns are the latest trend nowadays with children. In my view, designed three unicorn themed birthday decorations (that are all in my aid library , by this point). Children are fascinated by unicorns.

Design and sell the leather Earrings

Leather jewelry that is loved by many takes absolutely no skills in graphic design to create. If you're just looking to get your feet wet take a look at acquiring some unfastened leather swatches purchased from furniture stores and use the swatches to make your initial batch. My designs for these rings are in my helpful resource library.

Design and sell Felt as well as Fabric flowers

Cactus arrangement searches increased by 235% in the year 2019 Pinterest. Pinterest. Be succulent with succulents made of felt.

Design and sell Wood Letters

There are over one million searches per each month for Pinterest to find rustic hangings and signs. You can also cut wood using the Cricut Maker! Wood signs that are custom-designed are a sure bet.

Selling and Design Cards

Cards belong in their own category because they're extremely cost-effective to create, and there's a need to have one for every wedding, birthday, or anniversary. Additionally, delivery cards isn't cheaper than this.

Design and Sell Labeling Stickers for Sales

Labeling stickers are made to label items in the home. Items in the kitchen or pantry, classrooms, playrooms and many other areas can be labeled with labels stickers.

Design and Sell Labeling Vinyl

Labeling adhesive vinyl is designed to mark things within the home. Kitchen appliances and pantry, the classrooms, playrooms and many other areas can be labeled with labels vinyl.

Design And Cut Appliques

Fabrics with a lot of style can be made into appliques to create or decorate an area or item.

Create and sell Christmas ornaments

Christmas is a time when where people gather and decorate their homes, offices and places of worship and other areas.

Design and Sell Wall Decals

Wall decals in various styles are available to be manufactured available for sale at affordable and reasonable cost.

Design and Sell Doormats

Beautiful doormats can be created using the machine and then offered to clients. They can be made with either images or text. The doormats can be customized and offered for sale.

Design and sell kitchen towels

The kitchen towels are able to be designed and offered at reasonable prices. The towels can be designed using images or words of food items.

Chapter 9: Maintenance Of Your Cricut Machine

THe Cricut Cutter machine needs to be maintained through a variety of methods The blade needs to be replaced as well as the cutting mats have to be cleaned and the machine, generally, needs to be maintained clear.

Cutting Blade

Each blade you use could produce up to fifteen thousand cuts before needing replacement. To increase the number of individual cuts put the aluminum foil on the cutting mat, and then cut out several designs. This ensures the blade is sharp and extends the life for the cutting blade. The number of cuts made is contingent on the kind of material were removed by the knife. If you're working on many projects where thick materials must be cut, the blade will be damaged rapidly. It may also become damaged in the event that you cut a large number of items at high pressure. The best way to tell whether your blade should be replaced is when the cut quality begins to decline dramatically. In this case, it's recommended to change the blade. If you are replacing your blade it's recommended to purchase cutting blades made by the Cricut brand. Blades made from generic materials are not usually the highest quality and can make it necessary to change the blade. When installing the new blade after you've purchased the right one, you must first disconnect the Cricut Cutter machine. Make sure to unplug the machine prior to installing any thing in it. After that, you need to get rid of the old and dull cutting blade from the Cricut Cutter machine. After your cutting blade is removed, it's time to dispose of the blade. Locate the small silver button over the adjustment knob and press it down. This will release the blade. Be extremely, very cautious while doing this because cutting blades are extremely sharp, and may easily cut skin. Make sure that all blades are away from pets and children. For the installation of your new blade place the blade into the edge on the blade assembly to the left to the button for blade release. The blade will be lifted into the assembly. Reinstall the assembly into the machine, turning the machine around.

Join Cricut Access

If you're looking to make the most of uses from both the Cricut Explore machine and your Cricut Maker maker, we recommend you join Cricut Access now. There are two payment options. You can choose to pay a monthly cost of $10 or pay one-time for the whole year. This will be less expensive on a monthly by month basis. It will grant you the ability to access thousands of designs that are pre-designed and Cricut Access exclusive fonts, which you'd otherwise need to purchase. If you plan to make use of your Cricut often it will reduce your dollars instead of having to purchase each project an image separately. We all agree that it is much easier to pay a single price instead of trying to calculate what you're paying for projects. Make the most the Cricut and join Cricut Access.

Remove Your Cutting Mat

It is expected that the Circuit Explore machine will come with an blue 12"x12" standard grip mat for cutting. It is expected that the Cricut Maker machine will come with the white light grip mat.

You are aware that you'll put your cutting material on the mat prior to putting it in the cutter to be cut. As you'll discover that the cutting mat in green is extremely sticky , especially when it's fresh.

Keep your cutting mats covered

The cutting mats you buy to complete your projects will be brand new and come with a protective plastic sheet over it. The sheet can be removed and then put back on for the duration that the mat. It is recommended to keep the plastic cover for as long as you own the mat. It will help keep the mat at a good level on your mat, and makes the mat more convenient to store away when it is not being used.

Cutting Mat

The cutting mat, along with the cutting blade has to be maintained. The cutting mat may last anything from twenty-five to forty cuts. The lifespan of the mat may vary from this figure based on the force and speed of the cut that has been cut and the kind of material which have been made on it. To extend the longevity the mat take any debris off the mat following a cut and avoid scraping the mat. If you scrape your mat, it will push any debris deeper to the surface. After every craft it is recommended to use lukewarm water on the mat, then dab the mat dry using a clean towel. If the material will not stick to the cutting mat for any longer, it's time to change the mat. It is advised to buy several cutting mats and then rotate between them to increase the lifespan of all cutting mats. This will extend the lifespan of the mats since one mat won't be used across for several, numerous tasks in a relatively short duration. It is also suggested to keep every cutting mat as well as every cartridge and blades in an organised manner. Dispersing the parts in a random manner can cause them to break and degrade, which is why it is important to organize them organized in a well-organized way. One advantage of organizing the Cricut Cutter components organized is you will not lose or break the costly items which are essential for a variety of projects.

How to clean the Cricut Mat

It could also be based on the material you choose which can make your machine dirty. For instance the use of felt will mean you'll have to remove any small pieces with Tweezers. Another method to clean your Cricut is to apply an lint roller on the entire machine to remove scrap vinyl, debris and even pieces of felt. You can also put the roller on mats.

To wash your mats in the event that there is any left-over remnants left on your mats the best practice is to utilize the bleach or alcohol-free wipes gently clean the mat and clear it of grime dust, glue and dirt. There is also the option of purchasing GOO GONE. Spray this onto your mat and allow it to sit for 15 minutes. After that, utilize a scraper to scrape off the adhesive. This is only necessary in the event that your mat is filthy. In other cases, wet wipes can work.

Another trick to ensure your mats are tidy is to place the mats with a cover that protects them when you're not making use of the mats.

The Cleaning of the Cricut Machine

The final item to clear is the Cricut cutter machine. The machine must be cleaned with an damp cloth. Clean only the external panel of the machine without the machine being disconnected. Always clean the machine using dry, clean cloth following the cleaning of the exterior parts of the device. Don't use it with abrasive cleaners. Never clean the Cricut Cutter machine with abrasive cleaners like acetone, benzene and the other cleaners based on alcohol. Cleaning tools that are abrasive should not be employed for cleaning the Cricut Cutter machine either. Additionally, you should not submerge any of the components in the device or Cricut Cutter machine into the water since it could cause damage to the machine. Keep it away from the Cricut Cutter machine away from any liquids, food items or pets as well as children. Make sure to keep your Cricut Cutter machine in a clean and dry space. Also, don't place it in a place that is hot, cold, Cricut Cutter machine in excessive temperatures, extreme sunlight, cold or any place in which the plastic or other components of the Cricut Cutter machine can melt.

Cleaning and Maintenance

The maintenance of your device is essential, and you must be doing it frequently to ensure everything is in good condition. If you do not take care of your equipment, it's simply money wasted.

What can you do to take care of the machine?

Take your time when working with your machine. Keep in mind that it's an instrument, and it is important that you take your time to ensure that you keep it in good proper working order. Do not be rough with it as well, and when you work with machine components Don't be rough with them either.

The maintenance of your machine isn't only about ensuring that your parts don't get dirty, but you must be sure to keep everything in top operating condition.

Make sure your machine is on solid feet.

It may sound like a simple thing however, making sure that your machine is placed on level ground will allow it to make precise cuts every time. The machine's movement or wobbling may create unstable results in your work.

Make sure that no debris is trapped under the feet of your machine, which could cause instability before moving to the next step of troubleshooting!

Redo the entire Cable Connections

To ensure that the connections you have are optimal working condition make sure to disconnect every cable connections, blow into the ports, or use canned air, then connect everything securely back to the correct ports. This will ensure that all connections are communicating with one and are in the right places!

Completely dust and clean Your Machine

Your small Cricut does its best for you! Do your part by making sure that you don't allow dirt, gunk, dust or any other particles to accumulate on the areas and crevices. Adhesive is able to accumulate on the machine near the mat input as well as on the rollers. So be certain to concentrate on the areas that are affected!

Verify Your Blade Housing

Sometimes the debris and leftovers of your tools can get accumulated in the housings of your blades! Take them apart and clean any material that is accumulated that may cause a blockage to swiveling and motion.

Sharpen Your Blades

One of the most popular Cricut tricks employed is to attach a fresh, clean piece of foil onto your mat in Cricut, then use the blade you want to sharpen. By running the blades through the metal's thin layer helps to rejuvenate their edges as well as provide them with a bit of durability until the time comes to purchase new blades.

Cleaning the Machine Oneself

The exterior is relatively easy to wash - you only require a damp cloth. Be sure to never put any parts of your machine into water.

Always shut off the power prior to cleaning, just as you would for any other machine.

Sometimes, grease may build up and you might notice this on the bar of your cartridge in the event that you are a frequent user of cartridges.

Greasing the Machine

If you're in need of grease for your machine, first ensure that the machine is turned off, and that the intelligent carriage has been moving towards the left. Utilize a tissue to wipe it off, then shift your machine to its right side, repeating the process.

Then, you can move the carriage towards the center and then open an oil-lubrication package. Place a tiny amount on the Q-tip.

Don't use the cleaning spray directly onto the device due to obvious reasons. The bar that supports the housing should not be cleaned down, but if find excess amount of grease, ensure that you ensure it's washed to a high standard. Be sure not to be near the gear chain at the rear of this unit. Also, don't clean with the machine running, to ensure your security.

Cricut cutting machines are fantastic but you have to be sure that everything is in good order.

Chapter 10: How To Start Marketing Your Product

It is a common knowledge in the field of business that in order to earn money, you must first invest funds. That being said If you own an Cricut cutting device, then skip to the next paragraph, however, should you be debating whether it's worth it and you are unsure, read on. As we mentioned previously, Cricut has a range of cutting tools with distinct capabilities, and are offered in a diverse price. For instance, the Cricut Explore Air 2 is priced at $249.99 as well as Cricut Maker is priced at $399.99. Cricut Maker is priced at $399.99 (the older Cricut Explore Air model may be sold on Amazon at a cheaper cost). It is possible to buy one of these devices at a time of holiday sales, and get the bundle deal, which comes with a selection of tools, accessories and the materials needed for a trial project and a the opportunity to try a free trial of Cricut Access, you'd already have enough savings to justify the purchase for personal use. The best part would be to use the investment to make more money. There is always the option of purchasing more supplies as part of bundle deals or at the local stores for an affordable price. Overall the initial costs can be easily justified by the budgeted expenses for school projects which require you to cut shapes and letters, make customized gifts for your loved ones, and decorate your home with personalized decals, and , of course, your own jewellery designs. These are just a few of reasons to purchase the Cricut machine to use at home. Let's begin scraping away the pile of Cricut produced wealth to make you wealthy while having fun at work!

In this moment, let's suppose you've bought an Cricut cutting device and that you have enough experience with the easy-to-follow projects. You have the knowledge and tools needed to begin earning money from your Cricut cutting machine Let's get started on how to achieve this. These strategies have been tested and proven as effective strategies for making money that you can use without hesitation.

Selling Customized Pre-Cut Vinyl

Vinyl is a great beginner-friendly material that is easy to work with and comes in a wide range of colors and patterns that enhance its reputation. It is possible to create custom labels for glass canisters and containers to assist anyone who wants to arrange their pantry. Take a look at the trends in the internet and modify the labels to suit your needs. After you've got your labels created The simplest way to go about it is to start your own "Etsy" shop. It is completely free and easy to use. It's like the opening of your own Amazon Prime membership. If your product is popular there will be customers who purchase your product even without advertisement. However, if you wish to keep the pace high, consider advertising the Etsy listings on Pinterest as well as various other platforms on social media. This is a guaranteed way to increase traffic towards your Etsy shop and convert prospective customers to paying clients. Important to note is the photos you will use in your listing. You are not allowed to utilize any of the images available in Design Space. Design Space application and must utilize your own photos that are compatible with the product that you're selling.

Make a set of five or six names like sugar rice, salt, beans, oats, etc. which can be offered as a standard packager . You can also provide a custom-made package that permits customers to specify any specific word they want to be included in the package. Because these labels weigh nearly nothing, shipping can be accomplished using normal mail and usually one postage stamp subject to the delivery address. Be sure to not insist on the next day or two-day delivery option for these labels. Set aside enough time for delivery so that you can make and deliver the labels with no pressure. Once you've established your business plan, you can alter the cost and shipping costs of your product, but we'll get to that later. Look through similar Etsy listings to confirm that your price is competitive, and that you're attracting the right potential buyers.

Once you've gained an audience and you have a good reputation, you can provide additional vinyl-based products such as vinyl bumpers, iron-on or heat transfer designs that customers can apply to their clothing with an ordinary heating iron. Once you've established a following you can alter and personalize your offerings to become a one-stop shop for everything vinyl (great name for your new Etsy shop, isn't it?).

Selling finished pieces

You could be using your Cricut machines for a wide range of personal projects, including decorating your home, Christmas decor, personalized clothing and many more. When you are ready to embark on another of your creative adventures leading to original creations, simply create two versions of your creations and then add the second product for sale on the Etsy shop. Another advantage is that you'll be in a position to save every project you create in Design Space. Design Space application for future use. If one of your projects becomes viral, you are able to purchase the materials and transform into revenue-generating products. In this way, not only your initial idea to use it for personal purposes is paid for and you will earn more than you have invested in it at the very beginning.

Also, take some time researching what types of decorations and designs are popular in the marketplace and use them to fire ideas to your next design. The most popular trends in the market are customized cupcake and cake toppers as well as watercolor designs that can be used as impressive wall decor. Cake toppers are constructed using cards, which are a popular material for beginners, lightweight in weight, and could be easily shipped by tucking it into an envelope.

Customized Clothing and Accessories

T-shirts that have interesting designs and slogans are all the rage these days. Follow a similar strategy in the sales vinyl area, but go up a level. You can design sample clothes using an iron-on pattern and market it using "can be further customized without charge" and "transfer the design onto your own clothes" to gain traction on the market. Sling bags can be purchased and make them distinctive designs that can be sold as finished items with a higher cost than the standard sling bag.

Think about creating a line products that have a central theme such as that of the DC Marvel characters or the Harry Potter movies and design personalized t-shirts, hats as well as bodysuits for infants. You can design custom favor boxes for parties and gift bags upon the request of the purchaser. When your product is able to attract gained a loyal customers You can request project suggestions directly from them and provide them with a quote for the work. Aren't you impressed?? !

Chapter 11: A Look At Cricut Maker Machine

The Cricut Maker is an tool that can be a huge help in any and all phases of art work like sewing, scrapbooking, Party Scrap home Decor, Stamping, Custom Stationery Making Stamps as well as making EVA components and even assists those who work with painting so that you can create your own way of stenciling, truly customisable.

We will not only rely on the theories in this guide however, we will also demonstrate how to use the Cricut maker. That's correct. Let's get our hands dirty, set up your computer in order you can make the first cut. We will also demonstrate some of the innovative methods you can achieve this with this tool.

3.1 What do I need to know about installing Cricut Maker

Step one: Take the Cricut Maker from its box and examine all its parts:

* Power cable

* USB cable

The Blade Holder is a Thin Tip and Premium Blade. Holder is already installed.

*01 standard cutting base (Standard Grip) or Light Fixation

* (Light Grip) 30.5 cm by 30.5 centimeters (12 inches x 12 inches)

* Welcome Book

Materials for the very first project

1. Fine tip black pen

The software comes with 50 pre-built projects have been tested and are now time to select the location where your machine will reside.

For those who want When using it, be sure to set it up in a place sufficient to leave 25cm in the front and another 25cm behind.

Now, click"OPEN" and then press the "OPEN" button...

Wow!

As if by magic, an opening is before your eyes. You are able to go for the bucket because you have been swooning too much.

With great care, take off the seals and protective covers from every part you can find.

If you want to learn further about your Cricut Maker, notice that it features an Intelligent Panel on the right, which already includes all the settings to cut the commonly commonly used materials that we use in our daily lives. It also cuts more than 100 different materials but we'll get into this later.

In the center the central part has the two "drawers" to keep blades

and tools. Additionally, on the left there is a space for pens and tools. Additionally, there is an entryway for connecting physical cartridges which are still being used by those who purchased cartridges in this manner on older Cricut machines.

Once they're properly displayed, let's begin to install the Design Space, following the steps in the following steps.

3.2 How do I Set up Cricut Design Space

Access Design Space in your browser.

Choose the product you wish to configure or register. We'll select the "Creative Cricut Explore's Product Family" option.

Design Space is available for Android and iOS In addition, it is available for Windows as well as iMac. For mobile systems there's an offline edition of the software. On the computer offline version, it is only a beta version, and is not accessible to everyone.

TIP:

If your screen displays in different languages, it is possible to download Google Translate. Google Translate extension on your computer. This way, most of the process will be completely in English.

The next screen asks you to sign in using you Cricut account. If you don't have an existing Cricut

ID, create it by clicking on this screen. If, however, you already have an Cricut ID, simply click"Login" and then click on the "Login" option and then enter you login details and password.

After login, click "Download."

You must wait for the download to finish.

Once the download is completed Once the download is completed, when the download is complete, Cricut icon will be displayed in the file's name.

Simply click on"download" on the ".exe" download file and install it.

Follow the directions in the display.

Select "Finish." But, it's important to be aware that your device is automatically registered in its configuration.

Select "Continue".

3.3 How to connect your Cricut Maker Machine

It's time to connect your Maker and start it up.

If you'd like to connect to it using Bluetooth because it's already connected to Cricut Maker.

If you require assistance pairing your computer with Cricut Maker via Bluetooth, you'll see an explanation of the process at when you reach the conclusion of this article.

It can be completed at any moment so that we can continue with the connection using USB cable.

Once the machine is switched on, the process of installing is able to check if the firmware is up-to date or not.

After confirmation The next screen will give you the choice of registering for Cricut Access or not. It's the Cricut store which is where you will find thousands of projects, image files as well as fonts and stunning designs.

You are able to have a trial month to test it out and you can cancel or rescind your membership at any time or join in the future. If you choose not to subscribe at this point, don't be concerned.

There are a variety of free templates that you can use.

If you return to the topic the second screen shows where the whole thing begins, and you will be able to follow step-by-step all the directions in depth. Thus, you should use the tools and materials included with the machine: paper, Cricut black pen, and the blade.

Most importantly, you should follow the steps of the instructions and then make sure to add more details until you start to know the process of making an item. Very amazing. It's practical and gradual learning.

Let's continue to discover the accessories and the imaginative possibilities of the Cricut Maker.

3.4 Cutting Base, Cutting Blades , and Accessories

Let's now talk a about cutting blades, bases and other accessories you can put on your Cricut Maker, in addition to demonstrating some of the creative options.

* Cutting bases

There are four kinds of cutting bases and all can be utilized in Cricut Maker. So, when it comes to purging, each floor is colored to distinguish the glue's adhesion from the other. These are:

* Blue base = light fixation

* The base color is green. normal fixation

* Pink base is specific for fabrics

* Purple base = for heavier materials.

Important:

Purple Base Purple Base is not required to use Cricut Maker because it is specifically targeted towards materials with greater thickness which can be cut with Cricut Maker. Cricut Maker, but if you'd like to make use of it, it's fine.

* Cricut Cutting Blades

There are four different types of blades to pick from, the types of blades which can be used with Cricut Maker Cricut Maker are:

For materials with a thickness of 1.1mm:

Fine Point Blade (silver) is perfect to cut materials such as thin acetate, paper transfer, vinyl trace paper, other materials.

A premium-quality blade (slightly golden) is more durable and endurance than the standard Ponta Fina.

Fabric Blade (light pink) to be used for fabric with thinner layers. It's the same as that of the Ponta Fina blade, but the color of the holder is different so that you are able to identify the purpose of each. By doing this you can keep the cutting edge intact and increase the life of the blades.

Deep Cut Blade - For materials that are up to 1.7mm It cuts thin cork, EVA and other materials that are thicker with precision.

The process of changing the blades is inexpensive and easy, and even more so since once you've got an support in place, you will only require to purchase the tip, which is the blade, in actual.

Other accessories and tools can provide your pieces with an extra touch.

Do you know that perfect , continuous crease gorgeous to live in?

It is true that the Crease pen is the one responsible for everything. Its role is vital to fold folds in invitations, boxes, or give a unique details to a project. It is the support for "A" in the left side of the cart while the blade is supporting "B."

They can also be fantastic allies for your creative side. Much like the crease pen Cricut pens can be found within support of the "A" part of cart.

Cricut offers a variety of types that include: Fine point, medium point, that has sublimation ink and even a the ability to wash a fabric. Yes. You draw, stitch your work then wash it and then the paint comes out and the look you have created is flawless.

Cut by EVA?

Yes. Yes. Deep Cutting Blade makes it simple to work with more materials. There are many useful and simple bookmarks, however you can make more.

Conclusion

In in this book, we've given you the tools you need to help your Cricut perform at its peak all daylong. If you're able to master this, you'll be able to create anything you'd like because these machines cut efficiently, and are so versatile that can cause your head to spin. If you're still waiting to decide whether or not to buy your first device I hope this can help in making. We want you to have fun with Cricut Design Space, as well as thousands of other users across the globe.

Keep the tricks and tips kept close to hand as the reference guide so that you do not have to search for answer to your questions.

Design Space makes Cricut a cutter that is user-friendly and easy to use. I cannot emphasize enough how much you can benefit from the device as you become familiar with each procedure. If you're new to the game take it slow so that you don't become overwhelmed, and leave the machine before trying it out.

It is normal for beginners, so be sure to take your time reading this book before you begin on your very first venture.

Utilizing the Cricut machine isn't an unfamiliar experience for you right now. It is recommended to keep open to any new versions. Cricut always gives their users many choices to pick from, so make sure you take the time to do an extensive study of the products, materials, and subscriptions.

Utilizing the suggestions and tricks that are in this book isn't just going to assist you make use of your machine to complete any project that you desire however, it will assist you in making sure you have your equipment in top functioning in the best condition it is possible. A lot of the tips and tricks we've within this publication are suggestions that the majority of people wouldn't think of, but are very easy to implement, and will help make your machine last more time as opposed to having to test them all.

If you are able to follow the advice from this book, you can keep your equipment in top condition and complete projects to your heart's desire as well as becoming more knowledgeable. When you have the abilities you require to be able to move from basic projects to more professional ones which you'll be able to showcase your work at a retail store. Explore your passion and imagination and elevate this to the next step, with a project that is innovative and enjoyable. The machines are getting more and more popular rapidly due to the variety of items they can make. It's also a fantastic option to make gifts for your children or other family members and will make a huge difference in dollars in the future as the holiday season approaches. So, this device offers more possibilities and advantages than you expected.

Cricut Design Space is entirely user-friendly and simple to operate, and mastering it isn't a matter of thought. This is why I'm here to share some of my most beloved Cricut Design Space instructional exercises as well as tips and tricks for you! These will completely change how you live your Cricut life!

www.ingramcontent.com/pod-product-compliance
Lightning Source LLC
Chambersburg PA
CBHW071836080526
44589CB00012B/1015